ACTS OF THE HOLY SPIRIT

.

Other Books by Lloyd J. Ogilvie

Acts (Communicator's Commentary Series, Vol. 5)

Asking God Your Hardest Questions

Autobiography of God

Conversations with God

Creating Four-Part Harmony

The Greatest Counselor in the World: A Fresh, New Look at the
   Holy Spirit

The Heart of God: Daily Meditations on the Goodness of God

Hosea–Jonah (Communicator's Commentary Series, Vol. 20)

Lord of the Impossible

One Quiet Moment: A Daily Devotional

Silent Strength: God's Wisdom for Daily Living

ACTS OF THE

HOLY SPIRIT

GOD'S POWER
FOR LIVING

LLOYD J. OGILVIE

Harold Shaw Publishers
Wheaton, Illinois

ISBN-13: 978-0-87788-012-7

Edited by Mary Horner Collins and Pat Linnell

Cover design by David LaPlaca

Library of Congress Cataloging-in-Publication Data

Ogilvie, Lloyd John.
    [Drumbeat of love]
    Acts of the Holy Spirit : God's power for living / Lloyd J. Ogilvie.
      p. cm.
    Originally published: Waco, Tex. : Word Books, ©1976.
    ISBN 0-87788-012-3 (pbk.)
    1. Bible. N.T. Acts—Criticism, interpretation, etc. 2. Holy Spirit—Biblical teaching. 3. Christian life—Presbyterian authors. I. Title.
    BS2625.2.035 1999
    226.6'07—dc21   99-19007
                                                CIP

146625359

To Senator Connie Mack
"Without God we can't;
Without us He won't."

Contents

Introduction

The Holy Spirit Is Alive and Well

Well, it ain't me, Buster! thought Senator Connie Mack of Florida. We were approaching the end of the Bible study for senators one Thursday when I felt led to ask if anyone present needed to make a deeper commitment to receive fresh power from the Holy Spirit. The subject of our Bible study that day was "Commitment as the Key to Receiving the Renewing, Rejuvenating Strength of the Holy Spirit." I suggested, "Maybe there's someone here today who would like us to pray for him." Anyone who wanted to respond was invited to raise his hand and express the desire for prayer.

No sooner had the thought *It ain't me, Buster!* passed through Senator Mack's mind than he found himself raising his arm and saying, "I'm ready. I want you to pray for me." Looking back, the senator recalls having no idea what this would mean or what he would experience subsequently.

I asked Connie to move his chair to the center of the large circle of senators. His colleagues got up and gathered around him and, at my suggestion, placed their hands on his shoulders. One by one, they prayed for him. Then I asked three questions: Are you ready to commit your life unreservedly to Christ? Are you ready to commit your ministry as a United States senator to be a servant-leader? Are you willing to receive the Holy Spirit's supernatural gifts of wisdom, knowledge, discernment, vision, and prophetic power to boldly declare the truth as it is revealed to you? To each of these questions, Senator Mack responded with a resounding, "Yes." When he stood up, his face was radiant.

Many of the other senators said, "I should have been in that chair. I need the power of the Holy Spirit too!"

Senator Mack's recollections from that day are very significant:

> There is no adequate way to express the emotions of that moment, but as I looked back on it a few weeks later, I understood what was happening. I had a sense of something gushing out of me—my control of my life—and the beginning of turning over control of my life to God. I stress the word *beginning* because of what happened later.
>
> My wife, Priscilla, and I were in Vermont. It was cold and snowing. I enjoyed an afternoon of quiet reading—a book about the Holy Spirit as the greatest Counselor in the world. Later in the afternoon, I decided to go snowshoeing through the woods. Deep in the woods, I had an experience I'll never forget. It was so quiet. The only sounds were the branches of trees rubbing against each other.
>
> The gentle breeze was like the movement of the Holy Spirit. At that moment, I had this sense of prayer. I actually wanted to get down on my knees, but being a Florida boy and having snowshoes strapped on my feet, I wasn't sure if I got on my knees I could get back up. So, I stood there and lifted my hands to the heavens and prayed that God would fill me with His Holy Spirit. There was a sense of the infilling of the Spirit— love, joy, peace, patience, goodness, kindness, gentleness, faithfulness, self-control—and the feeling that I would be able to share these qualities with people I met.

Connie Mack's experience of giving up his control and accepting the control of the Holy Spirit was like opening a floodgate for the flow of power and the supernatural gift of leadership in his life. He had already been recognized as a good leader; now he has become distinguished as a great leader. This greatness manifests itself not only in his work as a senator but most of all in the way he reaches out to people across the spectrum, from fellow senators to custodians to police officers. He really cares for people of all kinds and stations.

Connie now leads our Wednesday morning prayer breakfast and rarely misses the Thursday Bible study. He is recognized as a spiritual person filled with radiance and resiliency from the Holy Spirit. What's great about this is that his strong political convictions have not been dulled by false piousness but have been strengthened with courage and boldness.

I have recounted Senator Mack's experience with the Holy Spirit at the beginning of this book to affirm that what we read about the acts of the Holy Spirit in the New Testament book of Acts still happens today. In fact, many leaders and staff here in the Senate family are currently enjoying a genuine spiritual reawakening.

We should not be surprised. Jesus promised that the Father would give us "another Helper" to abide with us forever. The Greek word for *another* in this John 14:16-17 promise is *allos,* meaning "another of the same kind." The Holy Spirit is like the Savior Himself in the present tense. He is One who, in addition to Christ, can do in our lives today exactly what Jesus of Nazareth did for people during His incarnate ministry.

Everything that Christ accomplished for us in His life, ministry, message, death, Resurrection, Ascension, and coming return as reigning Lord prepares us to be able to receive the infilling of the Holy Spirit. His death reconciles us; His Resurrection liberates us from fear of death, the future, and the power of Satan. His reigning authority is our sure hope that He will do for us what Peter proclaimed in his first sermon at Pentecost, "Therefore being exalted to the right hand of God, and having received from the Father the promise of the Holy Spirit, He [Christ, the Lord] poured out this which you now see and hear" (Acts 2:33, NKJV). This book will focus on a contemporary experience of what we see displayed on the pages of the book of Acts.

Jesus promised us another Helper. Various translations render the Greek word *Paraklētos* as "Advocate," "Comforter," "Counselor," and "Helper." This word, profound in its meaning, is associated with the one who is the counsel for the defense, who pleads a case on behalf of another. It also signifies a helper who stands beside a person to give encouragement in trial or aid in battle. John identifies Christ as our Advocate (1 John 2:1-2). He pleads our case before the Father on the basis of the atoning sacrifice of the Cross. But Christ promised another Advocate—another of the same kind—to be with us during the challenges and opportunities of our lives.

There are six major aspects in the ministry of the Holy Spirit. We will deal with these as they are revealed in the book of Acts. Now, for openers, allow me to delineate them for you. Doing so will give us a propitious promise of what the Holy Spirit can be for us today. It will also provide us with an inventory to evaluate whether we have received the fullness of the Spirit in all of the ways He seeks to be our Helper, Advocate, and Counselor, comforting us with exactly what we need to be courageous disciples in every hour.

Our Executor

The Holy Spirit is our Executor—the One entrusted with the responsibility of helping us to claim all that is ours through the life, death, and Resurrection of Jesus Christ. Savor Christ's own promise:

> But when the Helper comes, whom I shall send to you from the Father, the Spirit of truth who proceeds from the Father, He will testify of me. . . . When He, the Spirit of truth has come, He will guide you into all truth; for He will not speak on His own authority, but whatever He hears He will speak; and He will tell you things to come. He will glorify Me, for He will take of what is Mine and declare it to you. (John 15:26; 16:13-14, NKJV)

As the Executor of all that Christ has done and does for us, the Holy Spirit enables us to understand the true meaning of the message of Jesus. He inspires us as we read the Gospels. What Jesus said so long ago becomes His personal word to each of us now. It is as if we hear the Master speaking to our needs, our hopes, and our hurts. The Holy Spirit also helps us claim Christ's once, never-to-be-repeated atonement on the Cross as our own personal security. With His inspiration, we know that if you or I had been the only person in Jerusalem on Good Friday, Jesus would still have gone to the Cross for us. He helps us articulate the reflection,

> I sometimes think about the Cross
> And Jesus crucified for me;
> But even could I see Him die,
> I could not see a little part
> Of that great love which like a fire
> Is always burning in His heart.

And that's not all. Christ's last will and testament also includes an empty tomb and Resurrection power for every hour. Through the Holy Spirit, we can claim that as Christ lives we shall live also. Death will be only a transition in eternal life, which begins when we receive the gift of faith in Christ as our Lord and Savior.

Our Energizer
Jesus promised that the Holy Spirit would energize us. He promised the disciples and us that we would be endued (clothed) with power (Luke 24:49). He also promised, "You will receive power when the Holy Spirit comes upon you" (Acts 1:8). That's what all of us need. We need power to live what we believe, to do what love demands, to be bold and fearless disciples. The Holy Spirit is the Instigator. He gets us moving.

The Bible talks a lot about the strength of the Lord. That strength is the Holy Spirit. He gives us power to be hopeful thinkers, to have emotional health and resiliency, to do what we know is right and will bring ultimate good to everyone around us. The Holy Spirit is the Initiator of guidance and the Instigator of action.

Our Equipper
The Holy Spirit equips us with gifts for supernatural living. He

presses us to live beyond the limits of talent, experience, education, and erudition. He is our source for the fruit of the Spirit (remember Connie Mack's prayer?)—love, joy, peace, patience, kindness, goodness, faithfulness, gentleness, self-control. In reality, these are the qualities of Christ's character that the Holy Spirit reproduces in us. He actually changes our character and personality to be more and more like Christ's.

Added to that, the Holy Spirit gives us gifts for dynamic living and leadership (see 1 Cor. 12). A need before us will bring forth the Spirit's gifts from within: wisdom, discernment, knowledge, vision, healing and reconciliation powers, and the ability to see what God wants and then to proclaim it with expectation and boldness.

Our Encourager

The Holy Spirit is also our Encourager—the Spirit of love who helps us accept the amazing grace offered from the heart of the Father through the Son. The secret of lasting security is knowing that we are loved.

I've learned to take no one for granted. Beneath the most highly polished surface of the most highly placed women and men in our nation, there is often hidden insecurity. We all need to know that we are loved in spite of what we've done or said. The hidden scar of a loveless childhood is often creased in the folds of guarded memories. The blows of rejection during growing-up years shape our lack of self-worth. Some of us cultivate a cool facade; others develop bravado; still others become introverted. What we all have in common is a need to know we are loved. And here's the promise: "The love of God has been poured out in our hearts by the Holy Spirit who was given to us" (Rom. 5:5).

Our Expediter

Another of the Holy Spirit's assignments is to be our Expediter by guiding us to know and do the will of God. The one question I'm asked by leaders more than any other is how to know the will of God. The Holy Spirit is our Intercessor. He knows the will of the Father and makes the specific application of His will known to us.

It is in profound communion with the Holy Spirit on a consistent daily, hourly basis that we receive guidance for the direction of our lives and daily decisions. The more consistent that communion is, the more prepared we will be for the choices we must make.

In our Senate Bible studies and prayer groups, we spend a great deal of time talking about the importance of a daily time for silent listening to the guidance of the Holy Spirit for personal and professional needs. Silence is placed before intercession and supplication in people's ordered daily prayers. This is to overcome the tendency to call on the Holy Spirit only when we have crisis decisions to make. We're finding that consistent prayers for guidance provide ongoing clarity. We also know that the Holy Spirit opens doors, provides unexpected surprises, prepares people to be cooperative agents, and untangles the most complicated, seemingly unsolvable problems. We'll be talking a lot about this ministry of the Holy Spirit in chapter 7.

Our Equalizer

No list of the activity of the Holy Spirit in our lives would be complete without mentioning the powerful protective ministry of equalizing the influence of Satan. The Holy Spirit suits us up with the whole armor of God as outlined in Ephesians, chapter 6: He girds us with the belt of truth, the breastplate of righteousness, the shoes of the gospel of peace, the shield of faith, the helmet of salvation, and the sword of the word of God. Added to those is the confidence that comes when we pray for the protection of the Holy Spirit, who neutralizes the conniving strategies of Satan to hassle and hinder us with his self-condemning influence on our thinking. It is wonderful to know that the Spirit within us is greater than Satan who is in the world. The Holy Spirit is more than equal to overcoming the force of evil working around us in people under its malicious control.

These are only some of the ways the Holy Spirit works in our lives today. We will see how He worked in the apostles and early Church in the book of Acts. Then we will claim that same power for our problems and perplexities today. Our study of the book of Acts begins where it will conclude—in the sure conviction that though there are twenty-eight chapters in Acts, you and I are part of the twenty-ninth chapter being written all over the world. We are living in the most exciting time of history since Pentecost.

1
Preparing to Experience the Holy Spirit

Acts 1

There is a quiet desperation underlying the frantic lives of many people. They experience blandness in marriage, frustration at work, anger over the inability to change, and loneliness which has nothing to do with the absence of people. I hear the ache everywhere. Life is lost in living.

Most people I know want their lives to count. Their greatest fear is that they will become ineffective, inept, or insipid. They long for a challenge big enough to demand their allegiance, exciting enough to rally their enthusiasm, and crucial enough to warrant their time. Restlessness pervades both clergy and laity, an impatience with "business as usual" and a feeling of being powerless.

A man who recently retired confided to me, "Now I have all the time in the world, but I don't know what to do that will count." A woman in an unguarded moment of openness over a cup of tea asked me a disturbing question, "Do you think I have fulfilled the real reason I was born?" How would you have answered her? How would you answer for yourself wherever you are on the journey—young, middle-aged, or senior?

I believe these questions reveal a restlessness and stirring of the heart from God that is not being addressed by some churches today. Too often a church offers little challenge to people who may have been part of the church for years. Faith has been domesticated to suit our culture rather than dramatized as the ultimate purpose that gives meaning and direction to all else. But God is creating a sense of unfulfillment and dissatisfaction in His people. The Church must recognize this and offer a joyous fellowship to those who will write the next chapter in the book of Acts. We are not the embalmers of the past, but the enablers of the present and the empowered people for a new awakening.

What happened to the followers of Jesus, recorded in the first chapter of Acts, exposes our greatest need. That's why a study of Acts is so crucial to God's agenda for us today. If we dare to experience the same prelude to power that the apostles experienced between the time of Jesus' Resurrection and the gift of the Holy Spirit, we will be ready for a contemporary Pentecost, the rebirth of the Church, new fire for burned-out church people, and the formidable power of un-containable enthusiasm and excitement.

What Jesus did to get His disciples ready for the coming of the Holy Spirit at Pentecost is what He longs to do for you and me. Jesus took a confused, disunified, equivocating band of followers and forged them into a movement. Let's look at how He did it. Luke tells us vividly in the first chapter of his book entitled "The Acts of the Apostles."

Jesus Is with Us

First of all, Jesus wanted His disciples to be sure of Him as the leader of this new movement. Luke tells us that following the Resurrection, Jesus gave "instructions through the Holy Spirit to the apostles" and that He "presented himself alive to them by many convincing proofs" (Acts 1:2-3). Our Lord lived and taught among the disciples as the resurrected Savior. My study reveals that the words "instructions through the Holy Spirit" actually mean that Jesus taught them *about* the Holy Spirit. He wanted them to know that He was the same Lord who called them into discipleship, ministered among them, and was crucified and raised for them.

But Jesus wanted them to know something much more. He would always be with them through the Holy Spirit. They had to know this; they had to be sure. After Jesus ascended, the same Spirit who had dwelt in Him, whom they now experienced in this incisive interface of preparation, would return. The Holy Spirit would continue the Lord's activity among them through His living presence.

That's what we need to know. Christ is alive! He is here with us. He wants to come not just around or among us, but within us. The Holy Spirit is not some separate scepter, but the glorified Christ, alive and available. The remarkable "Acts of the Apostles" are truly *acts of the Holy Spirit* through the apostles. These acts are available today as part of everyday living for those who join Christ's movement to change the world.

God, Jesus, and the Holy Spirit?

There is a lot of confusion about the Holy Spirit today. We have fragmented the oneness of God. The same God who created all things, who called Israel to be His people, and who intervened in history in so many spectacular ways is the same Spirit who came in Christ to reconcile the world and who empowered the disciples at Pentecost.

Our statement of the Trinity should clarify our experience of one God: He is indeed our Father; we know this because of what He did for us through His Son; and we experience His presence in the Holy Spirit. No wonder the early Church alternately used the terms "Holy Spirit," "the Spirit of Jesus," "the Lord," and "the Spirit" when referring to the same reality. The Holy Spirit is the immanent and intimate approach to us of the living God whom we know through Jesus Christ.

The disciples needed to be clear about how Jesus would return, and so must we. Pentecost in our time will happen when we understand the Holy Spirit, long for the Holy Spirit, pray for the Holy Spirit, and open ourselves to the Holy Spirit as our contemporary with us and within us.

The Kingdom of God Is Real

The second step in Jesus' preparation of the disciples focused on the kingdom of God as the charter and message of the movement. The disciples were called to "proclaim the kingdom of God." In His message Jesus had clarified that the kingdom was within them, among them, between them, and was coming into the world through them. This kingdom means the rule of God over all life. All that exists, all that we have and are, and all that is to be must be brought under the Lordship of Christ. The movement into which the disciples were called was to become the kingdom on earth. It would not be a political kingdom, nor a return to Davidic glory, nor the Messiah's reign as temporal king of Israel.

As participants in the kingdom movement, we must allow the Lord to reign supreme in all our affairs and discover and implement the mandates of His teachings in every facet of our lives. There's a purpose big enough for any of us! What is there in our lives, in our churches, or in society that must be brought under the Lord's control and guidance? The answer to that question declares the marching orders for the movement.

A personal question now aches for an answer: How much of our lives are completely surrendered to God? What areas or relationships need to be opened to His guidance, forgiveness, and power?

Waiting for God's Timing

Next, Jesus addressed the *when* and the *how*—timing and strategy. Jesus wanted His disciples to become people who could wait for God, who would allow God to work through them, not people who would work for God on their own schedules and priorities. Can you imagine a more painful word to speak to these intrepidly urgent disciples than "Wait!"? They were ready to move! Christ was alive and victorious, and that was not the time to wait.

We all know how they must have felt. "Wait" is still the most cruel word for our impetuous natures to hear; yet there are ordained waiting periods during which our Lord prepares us for what He has prepared. It's sometimes difficult to wait for people to understand or change. Waiting for health in the midst of sickness is excruciating.

Waiting outside an operating room for a loved one's progress stretches one's faith. But waiting on the Lord is most difficult of all. We pray for guidance and direction, and we are forced to wait. Why? What is God up to? Then we realize that it's during the waiting times that He prepares us for the next phase of our lives in Him. Until we become fully dependent upon Him, completely open to do His will, and unreservedly willing to act on His timing, He cannot use us.

The apostles were told to "wait for the promise of the Father" (vs. 4). Jesus told them that this would happen when they were "clothed with power from on high" (Luke 24:49). Worth waiting for! Yet it's still difficult for us to wait; we want everything yesterday, or the day before that! But God is never off schedule: He is never ahead or behind time; He is always on time. We can trust that He will use all circumstances and eventualities for His perfectly timed plan for us. The people who share His movement in history must dare to believe that.

Baptized with the Holy Spirit

Jesus gave the qualification for initiation into the movement: baptism with the Holy Spirit. He reminds the apostles that John baptized with water. This outward sign of consecration, the experience of cleansing, became the initiation ritual for those who joined John's righteous movement. Now there would be a new kind of baptism. Just as John's baptism consisted of immersion in water, symbolic of cleansing, the Holy Spirit's baptism would require immersion in the very life-giving spiritual power of God. The apostles were to be indwelt, empowered, engrossed, and enlightened by the living Spirit of God!

Jesus knew that no one could become part of His kingdom movement and live the life He had lived without baptism of the Holy Spirit. Like many Christians today, the disciples knew Christ and were convinced of His Lordship, but they needed the indwelling power of the Holy Spirit. It's possible to be a believer and not have power; it's impossible to live the adventuresome life Christ intended without the Holy Spirit.

But the disciples weren't listening, nor are we. When they blurted out, "Lord, will you at this time restore the kingdom of Israel?" they displayed their ineptness and inability to listen. I am thankful for their poorly timed question, for it occasioned the Lord's teaching about how to trust God in the present and about what will be given to us for "now"-oriented faithfulness. The disciples wanted a return to past glory. Jesus helped them anticipate the future.

Jesus boldly explained it was not for them to know the times or seasons appointed by God. What they would be given was far greater. They would receive power when the Holy Spirit came upon them. It would mean *intellectual* power: they would have wisdom and knowledge. It would be *spiritual* power: they would have great faith and be able to do impossible things as miracles of the Spirit. It would be *emotional* power: they would have deep love for one another and other people in the world. And it would be *physical* power: they would have strength and endurance beyond their human potential.

Empowered to Be Witnesses

But now observe what follows. The power of the Holy Spirit will be given for a very specific purpose: to be a witness. The energizing, life-giving Spirit is for communication. A further preparation for Pentecost, then, is a commitment to be witnesses to and communicators of the grace and hope of the gospel.

The word *witness* actually means "martyr." There can be no Holy Spirit empowering unless we are engaged in being witnesses in the full implication of the word's original meaning. That implies that nothing can dissuade us from our belief and confidence in Christ. It also suggests a Cross-oriented love for the people with whom we want to share the good news of Christ's love. That precludes easy evangelism that is nonrelational and cares little for people's needs and growth. How many people in our lives know without any shadow of doubt our forgiving, accepting, and affirming love? Witnessing is not just spouting concepts or outlining plans for salvation. It means profound caring for and sometimes suffering with and for people. People are first on God's agenda. They are the focus of the movement into which we are called. The Holy Spirit is given so that we can be witnesses.

There are lots of people today who are seeking the gifts and power of the Holy Spirit for their own needs. That's only the beginning. The dynamics of the Spirit are given when we are involved in identifying with others and their struggles.

A woman wrote me to say that she had been in a dry spell spiritually. She was anxiously seeking the power of the Holy Spirit, yet she felt no flow of new life or enthusiasm. I asked her to tell me the names of ten people who needed love. Each one she listed needed wisdom, knowledge, and faith, which she could not engender in them. But when she became involved in some specific, costly ways of caring for these people, *then* the Holy Spirit empowered her. She realized that she was saying things to these people beyond her human intelligence and communicating hope beyond her experience. When she became stretched by the actual demands of loving, she received a profound experience of the Holy Spirit's gift of love. She knew it; so did the people she cared for. Her "martyrdom" did not cost her her life, but it did cost time, energy, and privacy. Her reward was an intensive, intimate experience of the Spirit of God. The same can be true for us. Who are the people on your list who need love?

Contemporary "Holy Spiritites," as I call them, want a private experience of the Spirit without pouring themselves out for people or giving themselves away to heal human suffering. Jesus is very specific about the dimensions of our witness. The resources of the Holy Spirit will be given in the realm of responsibility.

The realm of witness is delineated by the geographical extent of Jesus' challenge: "in Jerusalem, in all of Judea and Samaria, and to the ends of the earth" (vs. 8). For us that means at home, among our friends, at work, in the community, throughout the nation and the world. What a shock these areas of geography must have been to the disciples! Jerusalem? The Lord was crucified there! Judea? Where they were rejected! Samaria, among the impure half-breeds? The ends of the earth? Gentiles too? It would take years to assimilate that challenge. And yet, the further the witnesses extended, the more power from the Holy Spirit would be given. The same is true for us. No caring, no Spirit!

The Assurance of the Ascension

The next aspect of Jesus' prelude to power for the disciples was dramatic and decisive: He ascended into heaven. Jesus left them alone—a very startling way to teach! He had told them previously, "It is to your advantage that I go away, for if I do not go away, the Advocate will not come to you" (John 16:7).

How could His leaving them ever be advantageous? Look at it this way. He had to leave them in one dimension to return in an even greater demonstration of power. He left as Jesus of Nazareth, resurrected and victorious; He returned through the Holy Spirit, indwelling and ubiquitous. Now He could be unloosed on all the world. People would meet Him not just in Galilee, nor on the Mount of Olives, nor in Jerusalem, but everywhere throughout the world. He left as a risen Savior and returned as the mighty Lord of the Church, His movement to change the world.

Christ always "goes away," so to speak. That's how He forces us to grow. No previous level of growth or insight is sufficient. He will always leave us at one stage of discovery so that our security never rests on ourselves or on our own capacity to know him. The absenting Savior is constantly pushing us on to new frontiers. But He always returns in a greater discovery of Him than we ever imagined.

The angelic messengers told the confused disciples, "This Jesus, who has been taken up from you into heaven, will come in the same way you saw Him go into heaven" (vs. 11). Heaven here does not mean the reaches of the sky but the realm of God. It is not just "up there" but is a quality of relationship with God. From that realm Jesus would return in the Holy Spirit. He would come in the way He went: unpredictably, suddenly, powerfully. In that confidence the disciples left the Mount of Olives and went back to the Upper Room in John Mark's home where they had celebrated the Last Supper and where the resurrected Lord had first returned to them.

Unity in the Upper Room

It was there in the Upper Room that the disciples discovered the relational preparation for the movement. Note especially that they devoted themselves to prayer together. More than physical proximity, this means a spiritual unity. I have always felt that Pentecost happened not according to a date on a calendar but in response to reconciliation among the disciples. There were deep tensions among them during and after Jesus' ministry among them. Sharp divisions and conflicts surged among these strong-willed people. Until they were together on their knees, fully open to God and each other, the Holy Spirit would not be given. Notice that Jesus' mother and brothers were there. There had not always been appreciation and affirmation between them and the disciples or between them and Jesus. Now a remedial healing was taking place as a part of the prelude to power.

I have never known a contentious group to receive the Holy Spirit. Nor have I ever seen a church in which division and disunity prevailed receive the blessing of the Holy Spirit. If we want power from the Holy Spirit as individuals, we need to do a relational inventory: Everyone forgiven? Any restitutions to be done? Any need to communicate healing love to anyone? As congregations we cannot be empowered until we are of one mind and heart, until we love each other as Christ has loved us, and until we heal all broken relationships. The price seems high, but it's a bargain considering what can happen through Pentecost power.

Qualifications for Receiving the Spirit

The election held among the apostles to determine Judas's successor provides the final dimension for preparing to participate in God's work through the Holy Spirit. Two things stand out: the qualifications required to be a candidate and the expectant sense of destiny about the movement to which the apostles had been called. What was required for apostleship then is still basic for anyone who would receive the Holy Spirit today.

Acts 1:21-22 reveals that there were two qualifications necessary in order to become an "apostle": (1) they had to have been with Jesus from the beginning of His ministry, and (2) they had to have witnessed His Resurrection. For us today this means, first of all, an accepting of what God did through the life, ministry, and death of Jesus. Preparation to receive the Holy Spirit is a response to Christ's immeasurable love, which was dramatically imparted on the Cross.

Acceptance of Jesus Christ as Savior does not follow, but precedes, the baptism of the Holy Spirit. The first step toward Pentecost is toward Jesus. Until we have made an unreserved commitment of all we have and are, we cannot experience what He offers through the Holy Spirit.

Also, the Cross looms up between us and the power of Pentecost. Has the Cross been an experience of forgiveness for our sins? Have we accepted the assurance of atonement for the past, and have we been healed in the depth of our natures by His gracious love? Do memories haunt us? Are we imprisoned in guilt, self-justification, or defensiveness? The Holy Spirit is often sought by people who want to bypass Jesus and His Cross. It's like wanting a gift from someone, but not acknowledging or befriending them. It won't work. I have known countless people who have drifted into spiritualism or self-centered optimism who have sought the Holy Spirit without the message of Christ to guide their lives or the Cross to heal their personalities.

Equally necessary for apostleship and the baptism and filling of the Holy Spirit is the witness of the Resurrection. Of course, that does not mean that we have been in Joseph's garden at the tomb or in the Upper Room that first Easter morning. What it does mean is that we must experience and realize the Resurrection—not only Christ's but our own. That means several things. It means that we must accept God's power to raise Jesus from the dead. We must be people whose faith is rooted in that central miracle. Going further, it means that we must become people who joyously expect God's intervention in life's impossible situations. He is able to bolster our feeble efforts and do His best in what we think is the worst life can offer.

But now to the core of it. A witness to the Resurrection has gone through the death and resurrection cycle in his or her own life. Paul made it clear in Romans 6 that we must die to ourselves, our plans and purposes, our longings and dreams. When we surrender our own wishes and dreams, we become dead to self-centeredness. Then we can experience resurrection to the new life for which we were born and reborn. We become new creatures: the old person passes away and the new person comes alive. Only that kind of person has room for the indwelling of the Holy Spirit. Otherwise, the Holy Spirit has no place to dwell and no freedom to move within us.

A High Calling

A second aspect of the apostles' election of Judas's replacement that directly affects us is the need for the same sense of destiny the apostles had. They had been called to a very special movement and they expectantly awaited the power that God was about to pour out. When they prayed to God about their ministry and apostleship, it was with confidence and predestined assurance. They knew they were called, appointed, and set apart. And so should we. But don't forget, the Holy Spirit is given for apostleship, not for our pious enjoyment. We dare ask for the Holy Spirit because we too have an apostolic calling. Bold, intrepid, daring prayer results: "Come Holy Spirit, fill us, empower us, use us."

This is the amazing preparation for power Luke describes in Acts 1. No one need be restless, unfulfilled, or ineffective again. We have been selected to receive the Holy Spirit. A new day has dawned. We are ready for Pentecost.

2
The Dynamic Dimension

Acts 2

Recognition of spiritual emptiness is a blessing. Having a sense of need is a gift. The realization of the distance between who we are and who we can become is a special grace. The Lord is never nearer than when He excavates a sense of emptiness in us. The Holy Spirit can fill only empty hearts.

The apostles more than met this qualification for emptiness as they waited in the Upper Room during the ten-day interval between Jesus' ascension and Pentecost. Emptiness? They felt devastatingly insufficient. They had experienced a life of high adventure with Jesus. The power of God had been exposed in His message, healing, and love. Not even death could defeat that power. And Jesus had told them that same power would be theirs. The things He did they would do, and greater things. But now as they waited despairingly for the fulfillment of His promise of power, the words of hope seemed impotent and inadequate. It's a terrible thing to have a passion with no power.

Had it all been a dream? Did Christ really appear after the Resurrection? Were they victims of a wish dream? Ten days is a long time to wait when the frail thread of hope is stretched to the breaking point. Dejection was natural. They needed more than a revered memory or a remembered message. Only the Savior Himself would suffice. What good would an impersonal power be without Him?

Vision without vitality highlights our inability. We've all known it: a challenge to love when we have little capacity for it, a need to forgive others when we can't even forgive ourselves, a longing for wisdom and knowledge for life's demands when we can't figure out what to do with today, a desire to solve the unsettling needs of people when we have neither faith nor hope to believe that healing can take place. No wonder depression captured the emotions of Jesus' followers. It grew out of the desperate feeling that they could not be what they had been called to be.

What is it for you? What makes you depressed? Human nature, what people do or say, the suffering and sickness in the world? What is it that makes you feel the futility of life? Is it when you do your best and it's not good enough, when you try to make a difference and there is little discernible change, or when you love and little love is returned? I am convinced that depression is not circumstantial nor environmental, but deeply personal. It is rage turned inward upon ourselves as a result of the disturbing realization that we can't change things in ourselves, in other people, or in situations.

The mood in the Upper Room is shared by millions of people today, and I say, praise God! An evidence of His gracious love is that He has allowed us to come to this place of dejection so that we can be ready for Pentecost. Our efforts to live the Christian life on our own strength have run the long course of self-justification. Repeated commitments to care for people have left us exhausted and depleted. Programs to change society and bring justice have exposed our cherished cultural loyalties and forced us to admit that it's difficult to follow through on seeking first the kingdom of God when our security is up for grabs.

My own experience and my involvement with people have led to a deep conviction that may not be theologically orthodox but is experientially validated. There are two stages in becoming a vital Christian. One is our response to Christ through faith. We commit our lives to Him and begin to live for Him. We come to grips with His message and the lifestyle it demands. We try to love, forgive, and serve. Then, as a result of the demanding challenge, we are forced to admit that we can't do it; we don't have what it takes.

That prepares us for the second step, which must constantly be repeated. Out of power and conscious of our own failure, we are broken. Empty! That's the only way we can hear Christ's words, "Apart from Me you can do nothing." Only at that point can we accept the fact that being a Christian is not just following the Master, seeking to live up to a standard of perfection, trying to be faithful and obedient, but rather allowing Him to live His life in us and through us. That's what Pentecost is all about.

The Dynamic Dimension of Pentecost

Years ago when I was pastor of a small band of people in a new church, I used to greet people at the door prior to worship. As I shook hands with each person, I would ask, "What do you need this morning?" A casual observer would think the question ridiculous since many of the people were prosperous and successful. Yet a sense of spiritual need had brought them together to become an authentic church of seekers and strugglers. One morning a successful young lawyer grasped my hand and said, "I feel completely drained and empty. I need the Holy Spirit!"

That's what the disciples were saying on the Day of Pentecost in the second chapter of Acts. What happened first in the Upper Room, then in the temple courtyard, and finally in the temple courts was an encounter with, and an infilling by, the Living God Himself. They never forgot it. The experience was so dramatic that it changed their lives and gave birth to the Church. The disciples were given the dynamic dimension of the Christian life. Those who had followed Jesus in the flesh were filled with Jesus through the Holy Spirit. The same experience is available to us today. Picture it; feel it. Our own Pentecost can happen right now.

The rushing wind of the Spirit.

The disciples lifted their bowed heads and looked at each other with awe and astonishment. The still air was suddenly stirring in breezy gusts, then in a rush of mighty wind like the blast of a hurricane. A violent wind shook the room. The disciples staggered about trying to keep their footing, like sailors on the bow of a ship in a stormy, high sea. Something was happening, and the disciples were convinced that what they had been waiting for had begun. How gracious of the Lord to return in so unmistakable a way! The Spirit of the Lord—which the ancient Hebrews called the *ruach,* the "breath" of God—was now moving mightily among them. The tornado-like whirr was unmistakable. The echoing sound was like thunder.

The descent of tongues of fire.

The audible sign of the Spirit's presence was followed by a visible one. A lifelike manifestation hovered over the disciples; then suddenly it parted and over each of the disciples a portion flashed in the shape of a tongue, again a symbol significant to these Hebrew disciples. Fire represented the divine presence, a purifying and refining energy. They had been promised that they would be baptized with the Holy Spirit and with fire.

Now it had happened in a way to dispel their unbelief and coldness of heart. The fire they saw above each other's heads was confirmed by the fire of warmth and joy they felt in their hearts. That was what Luke meant when he said, "All of them were filled with the Holy Spirit" (Acts 2:4). What had come in undeniable, symbolic evidence now came within them. The emptiness was filled. The Lord took them where they were, as they were: broken, empty men who needed to be convinced by His presence without, so that they could receive His presence within. Here the word *filled* (*eplērōsen* in Greek) means that, as a container is filled with water, so their minds were actually energized with the Holy Spirit. New emotions were released and new volitional capacity engendered.

Praising God in other languages.

In an unexpected, outward expression of this electrifying of their inner beings, they praised God. But to their utter amazement they began talking in languages other than their native Aramaic—another sign of the miraculous presence of the Holy Spirit! They had heard other languages from Jews in the Holy City enough to realize that a magnificent linguistic capacity was now theirs. I can imagine Peter grasping Andrew to have him listen to his adoration of God in Latin and then to listen to John talk in pure Greek. Then other languages flowed with equal facility.

It was this, I believe, that sent the apostles rushing out into the courtyard and then to the temple. They wanted to tell about what happened and praise God in the many foreign languages represented in Jerusalem at the Feast of Pentecost.

Jews from all over the then-known world were gathered in Jerusalem to celebrate the Day of Pentecost. Many had traveled great distances to commemorate the giving of the law to Moses and to praise God for the ingathering of the harvest. The providence of God had been expressed in His guidance for life and the sustenance of food. Pentecost, fifty days after Passover, was a time for rest and celebration. The streets of Jerusalem, and particularly the temple precincts, were crowded with an international throng of Jews.

Luke is careful to enumerate the mixture of Parthians, Medes, and Elamites along with residents of Mesopotamia, Judea, Cappadocia, Pontus, and the Roman district of Asia. Added to these were Jews from Phrygia, Pamphylia, Egypt, and Libya. This list is topped off with both Jews and proselytes from Rome, Crete, and Arabia. That multitude represents a lot of different languages and dialects. And each individual heard about the mighty works of God in his own tongue. What a miracle of communication, both for the disciples and for the international listeners. The Spirit was at work in speakers and hearers at the dramatic demarcation of a new age.

Speaking in Tongues versus Other Languages

I would like to digress long enough to clarify a point. The Scripture says that the apostles spoke in *other* tongues or "other languages" (vs. 4), not that they spoke *in* tongues. The gift of tongues—an ecstatic and unbridled expression of praise in an unintelligible language—was a later manifestation of the indwelling of the Holy Spirit.

Luke makes reference to this gift in two subsequent incidents in Caesarea—when Peter preached at Cornelius's house and at Ephesus when Paul laid hands on a band of disciples of John the Baptist. Paul lists speaking in tongues and interpretation of tongues as specific gifts of the Holy Spirit. His Corinthian letter acknowledges the authenticity of the gift but cautions about its misuse.

Interest in the gift of tongues in our own day is great, and many people have found delight and release in it. Its public use, with interpretation, allows the prophetic power of God to guide the assembly of His people with a supernatural imparting of wisdom. Privately, a person may pray in tongues and then be given the gift of insight into what God is seeking to communicate. Both manifestations are legitimate gifts, but never to be flaunted or used as a basis for self-justification before God or others.

In my opinion it is wrong to believe that speaking in tongues is the only undeniable sign that we have received the Holy Spirit, or to use the term "charismatic" to describe it. *Charismatic* means "gracegifted." The Greek word *charismata* refers to all the gifts delineated by Paul in 1 Corinthians 12. On Pentecost it was not speaking in tongues that was given but the gift of communicating praise to God for Christ in other languages.

For the disciples and for all those who heard, the manifestation of speaking in foreign tongues on the Day of Pentecost declared the universality of Jesus. Concretely, the Great Commission to go into all the world was part of the enacted miracle of Pentecost.

What Is Our Reaction to Pentecost?

Response to the miracle in Jerusalem was very interesting. People were amazed and perplexed and asked each other, "What does this mean?" Others mocked, saying that the apostles were drunk. Still others, as we shall see, were alerted to the possibility that God was indeed present and doing a new thing. They listened to Peter's speech that followed, and three thousand of them were converted.

We need to pause and regroup our own personal responses to all three manifestations of the outpouring of the Holy Spirit on Pentecost. Wind, fire, and the gift of communication through praise and prophecy are all part of what happens when our emptiness is filled by the Holy Spirit.

The wind of Pentecost begins with God.

The Holy Spirit was not created by God for Pentecost. This was not some new aspect of God revealed and released for the first time. The Holy Spirit is the essence of the eternal God, Creator and Lord of all creation, the same Spirit who dwelt in Jesus and is now given to indwell those who believe in Him.

We are at the center of truth when we say that the Holy Spirit was and is the gift of the resurrected, ascended, reigning Christ, now among and within His committed followers (vs. 33). Jesus had promised the infilling gift: "The Father and I shall make our home in you. Abide in me and I in you." Later Paul expressed the central reality of the Christian experience when he said, "Christ in you, the hope of glory." The wind, the breath of God, the living Christ, the Holy Spirit are one. Just as a newborn baby is enabled to breathe in the breath of life by the skilled tap of the obstetrician, so too, we breathe in the Spirit and become new creatures.

There's a lot of talk about whether we receive the Holy Spirit at conversion or as a second blessing later on. The question is distracting and confusing because it's based on a fallacious fracturing of the unity of God. All aspects of our conversion, rebirth, infilling, and growth are works of the Holy Spirit. His gift of love frees us to admit our need. His gift of faith enables our initial response to the gospel. His persistent presence liberates us from the idea that we could ever live the Christian life on our own steam.

Each time we acknowledge our inadequacy, the Holy Spirit fills our emptiness with particular gifts we need to carry out Christ's mission and ministry. When the needs of the world break our hearts and the triumphant adequacy of the gospel grasps our minds, we are being baptized by the Holy Spirit.

The baptism of the Holy Spirit is not an esoteric, special, or separate experience given to a chosen few believers. The Holy Spirit is utterly available. But if we are filled with our own pride, plans, determination, and self-effort, there is no room left. And if we are attempting only those things we can do on our own strength, who needs the Holy Spirit and His gifts? When we get fed up with being filled by the things that do not satisfy or empower, we are ready to be filled with the Holy Spirit.

The fire of Pentecost galvanizes our faith.
Flames of fire describe what happens when the Holy Spirit takes up
residence in us. Potent words flow in explanation: conviction, passion,
enthusiasm, galvanization. All of these are part of the fire of the Spirit
in us.

The disciples on the road to Emmaus after the Resurrection spoke
of their hearts "burning within them"—a foretaste of Pentecost. John
Wesley described his conversion as a time when his heart was
"strangely warmed." Christians have been called the "fellowship of
the flaming heart." Jesus promised that the Holy Spirit would bring
to mind all that He said and did. And what He said and did was
inflammatory: the Word of God, forgiveness and reconciliation, defeat
of death, Resurrection, the offer of new life now and forever. These
convictions—springing from a passionate devotion to Christ and the
world He died to save—offer the only explanation for the courage
and daring of the early Church and believers ever since. The fire of
love leaps out of us and sets a fire burning in others. Warmth of
countenance, expression, and words are authentic signs that the Spirit
lives in our hearts.

But there's more to the fire of the Holy Spirit. It also purifies and
galvanizes. John the Baptist's promise that we would be baptized with
the Holy Spirit and with fire carries serious implications. "His win-
nowing fork is in his hand, and he will clear his threshing floor and
will gather his wheat into the granary; but the chaff he will burn
with unquenchable fire" (Matt. 3:12). This passage not only refers to
what happens to those who do not believe, but also what happens
to those who do.

The fire of the Holy Spirit burns out the chaff in us. Our chaff
is anything that keeps us from our Lord or any other person—attitudes that cripple, values that demand false loyalty, the habits that
incarcerate us. Our chaff also includes memories of past failures
that we refuse to forget and plans for the future that could never
receive our Lord's blessing. Most of all, our chaff includes willful
self-centeredness and determination. We are loved just as we are, true,

but the Spirit will never leave us there. His work is to re-create us in the image of Christ. Once He comes to live in us, He begins to move into every area of our minds and hearts. He's never finished with us.

Some time ago I passed through a very difficult and painful period of seeing myself realistically through the eyes of a couple of people I love very much. They pointed out a developing pattern that could cause ineffectiveness in my relationship with them, and possibly with others. The only place I could go with this data was to prayer. The Spirit was firm yet gentle. He confirmed aspects of the criticism and helped me see the insecurity that prompted the pattern. Then He gave me power to do something about it. The amazing thing was that just before this need for change was brought to my attention, I had been feeling very secure and at peace, as if my growing in Christ had finally reached a quiet maturity. Not so! Chaff I hadn't realized was there had to be burned away. And it will be like this for as many years as I have to live on earth. Under the fire of the Spirit the dross will surface and have to be skimmed off to make the metal pure.

Closely related to the burning of chaff is the galvanizing of our relationships by the fire of the Holy Spirit. Welding takes white-hot fire, and so do deep, inseparable relationships. The fire in my heart coupled with the fire in yours makes us one. The union is intellectual as we receive the mind of Christ; it's emotional as we feel the warmth of love for each other in spite of hurts and failures; and it's volitional as we make decisions to do His will together. Christ prayed that we might become one. The living Spirit in us is indefatigable in making that possible.

Praise is evidence of the indwelling of the Spirit.
The third aspect of Pentecost is praise. We must never be so distracted by discussing the gift of speaking in tongues that we miss what the apostles talked *about* in many languages: the mighty works of God, His "deeds of power" (vs. 11).

Praise is the antidote to pride, the evidence that we have accepted the fact that all we have and are is a gift. More than that, praise unlocks further power from the Holy Spirit. If we praise God in good times, the Spirit heightens our joy. If we praise God in difficulties, we acknowledge that He can work in all things. Praise is surrender: it is thanking God that He can use everything to enable us to grow. Most of all, praise is a universal communication.

The finest way to share our faith is to tell others about what God is doing in our lives, but not just the successes. When we praise God in the midst of frustration and pain, our witness is undeniable. At one Wednesday morning Senate prayer breakfast, Senator John Edwards shared with us how he recovered true intimacy with God through the grief he felt at his son's death. John is a relatively new senator, but he forged a deep bond of friendship with the other senators through his honest vulnerability. Several other senators had endured grief over the loss of loved ones; they identified with him and were strengthened by Senator Edwards' forthtelling and praise of what the Lord had done for him.

The apostles' eager, impassioned praise brought the charge that they were drunk. Peter's response occasioned the first Christian sermon to explain the new quality of life available in the Holy Spirit. Wouldn't it be great if contemporary preaching routinely disclosed such winsome witness that people would want come to experience that same amazing life in the Spirit?

Peter got the question of new-wine excitement out of the way quickly. "Now, listen; you know what time it is," he implied. "It's only nine o'clock in the morning [the third hour of the day]. We haven't had anything to eat yet because we have not yet made our sacrifices; that's another hour away and our main meal is two hours beyond that. We don't have wine without a meal. How can you be so absurd as to think that we are drunk? Something else has happened. Let me tell you about it."

Immediately Peter repeated the prophecy of Joel written about 400 B.C.: "And in the last days I will pour out my Spirit upon all flesh." That's what was happening in Jerusalem! The result, according to Joel, would be that "they shall prophesy" (Acts 2:17). These were not to be the wild, ecstatic mutterings of the prophet bands of ancient Israel, but prophecy focused in visions and dreams of what God would do.

Prophetic proclamation comes from the Spirit.

The fourth evidence of the Holy Spirit's power then and now is prophecy. This is not just foretelling but forthtelling, a proclamation of truth. The Holy Spirit enables us to see things as they are, Christ as He is, ourselves in His light, others in their need. The gift of prophecy is the capacity to communicate truth with daring freedom and boldness. It's not accusing people for who they fail to be, but sharing who they can become. The Spirit gives us discernment about what to say and the courage to say it with love.

Without the Holy Spirit we will constantly be in trouble, saying too little or too much. A man told me once, "There are times I wish God would give me lockjaw. I always say the wrong thing when I try to help people by sharing my faith." We talked and prayed about this together, asking for the specific gift of prophecy. The Holy Spirit, not a stingy giver, gave the man sensitivity and empathy. He learned how to listen and watch for the Spirit's opportunity and judge when the time was right. Later, a man with whom he worked began going to church. Subsequently, his conversion and new life were a direct result of my friend's gift of prophecy, his forthtelling of what Christ meant to him.

Peter not only explained the effusion of enthusiasm as a result of the Spirit being poured out; he went on to use the gift of prophecy himself. The gospel he presented served as a pattern for subsequent preaching in the early Church. He proclaimed what God had done in Christ; then he fearlessly explained what his people did with what God had done. Finally, he passionately communicated what God did in spite of what they had done. The life, death, Resurrection, and power of Christ were undeletable elements of early Christian preaching.

No wonder Peter's prophecy generated the results it did. People were cut to the heart and cried out, "What should we do?" Peter's response has never been improved upon in centuries of explanation of how to become a Christian: "Repent, and be baptized every one of you in the name of Jesus Christ so that your sins may be forgiven; and you will receive the gift of the Holy Spirit" (vss. 37-38). Peter asked for nothing less than for people to turn around, accept Jesus as Messiah and Lord, confess their sins, be baptized, and fearlessly become identified as followers of the Master. As a result, they would receive the Holy Spirit. Three thousand responded. The same Holy Spirit who had filled the apostles now gave the gift of faith to the new believers.

A New Fellowship Is Born

The final manifestation of Pentecost outpouring was the fellowship of the Holy Spirit. "All who believed were together and had all things in common; they would sell their possessions and goods and distribute the proceeds to all, as any had need" (vss. 44-45). The Church was born. A new humanity came alive. God's eternal strategy for reconciliation between Him and His people and of His people with one another was fulfilled. Eden revisited, Mount Moriah superseded, Exodus accomplished, a new temple not made with hands, Calvary's sacrifice realized, Resurrection victory shared, the Holy Spirit gift accepted, a new Israel—the Church—was born.

The Church of the Holy Spirit is the historical demonstration of God's eternal purpose for all people. There can be no true fellowship without His living presence in us and between us. The people in whom the Spirit lives are broken open to become channels of grace to fellow adventurers in Christ. There is no need I have ever heard articulated that could not be met by the Holy Spirit. When He fills us, the fruit of the Spirit intuitively engenders love, joy, peace, patience, kindness, goodness, faithfulness, gentleness, and self-control in our characters. What else do we need? The greatest gift of all—the Lord Himself! And that relationship is available through the communion of the Holy Spirit.

The Day of Pentecost began with the disciples together in one mind and heart. The Holy Spirit could come because of that unity. By the end of the day the fellowship had expanded by three thousand. Luke ends the second chapter of Acts with triumphant joy: "And day by day the Lord added to their number those who were being saved." The movement to change the world had begun, and we have never heard the end of it.

3
The Liberating Spirit
Healed and Whole

Acts 3

The birth of the Church in Jerusalem created a community of people through whom the Lord could continue His ministry of reconciliation and healing. A new age was born; Christ was alive in His people, and they were now equipped to do the things Christ Himself had done—communicate His love and bring people to Him. No sooner had the Holy Spirit been given than they were confronted by human need in the form of the paralyzed beggar at the temple gate.

It always happens that way. The immediacy and intimacy of the Holy Spirit galvanizes us into oneness in the body of Christ, the Church. Then we realize that the Church was born to be a blessing. The wind of the Holy Spirit carries us to people in need. The fire of the Holy Spirit kindles warmth and affection for others. This consuming fire burns out the chaff of judgmentalism, reserve, and exclusivism. The passion of Pentecost releases excitement and compassion for people.

But the rapture of Pentecost comes with responsibility. The tragedy is that many who are delighted by Pentecost are not ready for the demands of caring for people. We want to linger in chapter 2 of

Acts, enjoying the Holy Spirit and other Spirit-filled people. But such eccentric exclusivism will release little of the Spirit's energizing power for the mission of Christ in the world. The result is a subculture with its own jargon and religious games. The qualifying questions are often, "Are you filled with the Spirit?" or "Are you charismatic?" The questions should be: "Has the Spirit drawn you to people in need?" "Have the gifts of the Holy Spirit equipped you for ministry?" "Is the fruit of the Spirit communicating Christ's love, joy, and peace to others?"

Power for Paralysis

The authentic test of Pentecost is revealed in Acts 3. We must stand, as it were, with one foot in chapter 2 and the other foot in chapter 3 or we will not be able to walk with the Lord effectively. We need to discover how to use the power and passion of Pentecost to affect and cure the paralysis of the world around us.

Acts 3 tells us that Peter and John were on their way to the temple to pray at 3:00 P.M. On the way they met a lame man who was brought each day to beg money from those entering the temple to worship. The contrast of the Beautiful Gate and this pitiful paralytic must have been arresting. According to the ancient Jewish historian Josephus, the gate was fifty cubits high. He says, "It was adorned after a most costly manner, as having much rich plates of gold and silver." Made of Corinthian bronze, it was shaped in the form of a vine symbolizing Israel as the vine of God in the world's vineyard. It shone like gold in the sunshine, but the radiance of the metal was nothing compared with the Holy Spirit-filled radiance of Peter and John, who were living branches of the true Vine, the Messiah Himself. They were incarnate intimations of the promise the Lord had made, "Those who abide in me, and I in them bear much fruit" (John 15:5).

Little did the lame man know that he would become the fruit the Lord had promised. He was immediately drawn to Peter and John. The Holy Spirit's love and joy were flashing from their faces. "Surely those two will give me some money," he may have thought as he called to them.

Sensitized with the empathy of the Holy Spirit, Peter and John had new eyes to see human suffering. The Spirit's gift of love and compassion pulsed through them as they looked intently at the beggar. The crowds swirled past them through the gate, but Peter and John were riveted on the paralytic as if he were the only person in Jerusalem. The beggar importuned them, reaching out his imploring hand in the hope of receiving alms. Peter's response has echoed through history as both prognosis and prescription. He told the beggar that they did not have what he wanted but what he needed. "I have no silver or gold, but what I have I give you; in the name of Jesus Christ of Nazareth, stand up and walk" (Acts 3:6). He did not offer him fortification for his begging life, but faith for healing and the beginning of a new life.

The Greek wording here conveys that Peter seized the man's hand and raised him up. Immediately the beggar's feet and ankles were made strong. What a vivid picture Luke gives us of those three on their way to worship: Peter and John filled with the joy and excitement of the living Christ through the Holy Spirit at work in them; the healed paralytic expressing uncontainable exuberance. "And he entered the temple with them, walking and leaping and praising God" (vs. 8). He leaped with liberty, dancing to express his delight.

Bringing It Home
Now let's ask a question that puts this first miracle of the Spirit-filled disciples into a personal context that makes the whole passage so much more compelling. We must ask, "Who does the lame man represent to us?" He may represent one of three persons or possibly all three at once.

Some of *us* are like the lame man. We have an immense immobility—physically, emotionally, or interpersonally. We are acutely conscious of our inabilities, inadequacies, and ineptnesses. We want to love, but it's difficult. We want to express care, but we can't get free of ourselves. We long to live a significant life, but we are cornered by circumstances and people who hold us back.

Ever feel paralyzed in body or spirit? Is your greatest need right now most like the lame man's? You need more than gold or silver; you need healing! If that's where you are, let the full impact of this passage inspire you. What happened to that man by the Beautiful Gate is the beautiful gift God wants to give you also.

Others who read this may know a person who needs healing. For these people the passage thunders a question: "Why is it that I have silver and gold to offer, but have never dared utilize the power of the name of Jesus to bring healing?" We all know people who need Christ more than they need anything our silver or gold can buy. To read and study this passage honestly, we must do what Peter did—we must direct our fixed attention on them. The power of Pentecost is for these very people, through us.

For others, the passage will bring to mind the public paralysis all around us. By public I mean social and cultural paralysis that results from structural and corporate evil in our society. If we care deeply about people, we must reach the taproot of pollution in our communities and nation. How should we pray? What should we do? The amazing thing is that we already have both the power of the name of Jesus and the silver and gold He placed at our disposal to heal human suffering. What have we done with either?

I hope this discussion has brought three things into focus: (1) the paralyzed dimensions of your own being that need healing; (2) the people who need Christ's healing through you; and (3) the evils in our contemporary life that paralyze people with injustice or inequality. What we will discover next will empower us for all three. Keep them focused in your mind.

A Split-Second Miracle

This powerful chapter of Acts can be divided into three sections. Acts 3:1-10 deals with *what* actually happened; verses 11-16 shows us *why* it happened; and verses 17-26 reveals *how* the same thing can happen now. Study this chapter for the full impact of what the Lord wants to do with the paralyzed parts in us and in the people around us.

What actually happened that day in Jerusalem? Luke, the physician, uses very specific medical terms to describe the paralytic's congenital difficulty. The Greek word for feet refers to the base or heels; the word for ankle bones refers to the socket for the ankle and the heel. Thus "leaping up" describes a sudden socketing of the heel and ankle.

The bones had been out of place, and a joining or linking occurred. The language indicates that the healing process, which would normally be corrected by a physician only over a long period of time, happened in a split second.

Note the elements of the healing. Peter looked at the lame man intently, prayerfully, as if seeking discernment from the Spirit. Then he proclaimed the name of Jesus Christ of Nazareth as the agent of healing. In that day, the *name* of someone actually carried the authority, power, and availability of the person named. It was as if Peter had said, "The authority of Jesus over sickness, His power to heal human affirmities, His presence here with us now—by that, rise and walk!"

In addition, Peter took the lame man by the hand and helped him up. He made personal contact. Then the two dynamic forces combined—Peter's Spirit-filled lift and the Spirit of life working harmoniously. Both are necessary for healing; the Lord has deemed it so. Today, the Holy Spirit, the divine Healer, still is available through Pentecost-powered, willing, expectant, trusting people like you and me.

Jesus Revealed as Messiah

The people's amazement at the healing prompts a second question: Why did this happen? The Scripture is clear that Peter and John and the healed man went into the temple to worship. The prayer service took about half an hour. Can you imagine what praise and adoration must have surged from their hearts? The prayer time gave Peter an opportunity to contemplate the startling, explosive truth that the healing miracle conveyed. The purpose of Pentecost must have pounded through his thoughts: *Christ is still alive! He has come to live in us in the Holy Spirit. He is now ready to do through us what He did among us in His ministry. There is something about that name—Jesus. Savior. Healer. All the power of God that we witnessed in Jesus is available to us!*

While the three prayed, crowds outside were buzzing with rumors. "You know the beggar who is always at the Beautiful Gate? Lame since birth. Well, we saw him walk and leap and praise God! How did it happen? The disciples of the crucified Jesus of Nazareth used His name to heal this man!" No wonder there was a great crowd waiting for them at Solomon's portico when they came out from evening prayers.

Peter wanted to make two things undeniably clear as he began to preach. First, there was no human power in him or John that made the miracle possible. He wanted to take the attention off the human agents of power and rivet the crowd's attention on the Power Himself. To do that he pointed them to the God of Abraham, Isaac, and Jacob. They should not be amazed or surprised by what God had done that day; it was but one more in a succession of miraculous interventions for His people through Israel's history.

The second startling truth Peter communicated was that the God of Israel had come in the Messiah, Jesus of Nazareth, whom they had crucified. What Peter preached was a refined Christology engendered in him by the Holy Spirit. The things the Spirit had revealed to him on the road to Caesarea-Philippi, intensified by the experience of the Transfiguration and confirmed by the power of the Resurrection, were now punctuated by the exclamation point of Pentecost. As G. Campbell Morgan puts it, "In half an hour after Pentecost, they knew more about Jesus than they had ever known before."

The Spirit had taught Peter well, and now he could use cherished messianic Scriptures to drive home his point. Jesus was the holy and righteous One predicted in Isaiah 31:1 and 53:11; Zechariah 9:9; and Psalm 16:10. He was the servant Messiah of the Old Testament prophecies (Isa. 42:1-9; 49:1-13; 52:13–53:12). Yahweh had come in Jesus, whose name means "salvation from sin." The Spirit of the Lord was upon Him, and by the same Spirit He did mighty wonders. The Spirit who raised Him from the dead was the same Spirit they had just seen at work in the lame man.

Peter's Christology takes on glorious illumination through the guidance of the Holy Spirit. He calls Jesus the *Author of Life* (vs. 15). Other translations of this passage use the expressions "Pioneer of Life", "Prince of Life", and "Guide of Life". John, who was standing by Peter that day, put the same truth in arresting terms when he later wrote his Gospel:

In the beginning was the Word, and the Word was with God, and the Word was God. He was in the beginning with God. All things were made through Him, and without Him nothing was made that was made. . . . And the Word became flesh and dwelt among us, and we beheld his glory, the glory as of the only begotten of the Father, full of grace and truth. . . . And of His fullness we have all received, grace upon grace. (John 1:1-3, 14, 16, NKJV)

That Scripture carries the deep meaning of Jesus as Author of Life. The full implication is "file leader," one who takes precedence, one who goes first. What that means to us is that the creative power of God who made the world—the divine *logos*, the Word of God—is also in the One who came as Messiah. He is the Source of both life and salvation. As Author of Life, He is Originator, Leader, and Example. Hebrews 2:10 catches the same spectacular truth: "It was fitting for Him, for whom are all things and by whom are all things, in bringing many sons to glory, to make the *Author of their salvation* perfect through sufferings" (NKJV, italics added).

In the light of this truth, Peter explained: "And by faith in his name, his name has made this man strong, whom you see and know; and the faith that is through Jesus has given him this perfect health in the presence of all of you" (Acts 3:16). The name of Jesus carried all the power of Creator, Messiah, and resurrected Lord. The name of Jesus released all the power of the Holy Spirit. By invoking Jesus' name, His power and authority were called into action and mediated by His living presence through the Holy Spirit.

The miracle of the healing of the lame man was accomplished with the power and authority Jesus gave the disciples near the end of His ministry:

Very truly, I tell you, the one who believes in me will also do the works that I do and, in fact, will do greater works than these, . . . I will do whatever you ask *in my name*, so that the Father may be glorified in the Son. (John 14:12-13, italics added)

That's what Peter and John did that day at the Beautiful Gate. By the name of Jesus, the Author of Life, the lame man was healed.

Faith to Respond

But who had faith in the name of Jesus? Peter and John or the lame man? The answer to that is crucial for the needy people we discussed earlier. *The Living Bible* gives us the very crucial answer in Peter's explanation: "Faith in Jesus' name—faith given us from God—has caused this perfect healing." It was the faith of Peter and John in Jesus' name that enabled the release of God's healing power.

That leaves us with an amazing realization: We have been called and chosen, given the freedom to accept the love and forgiveness of the Cross, empowered by the infilling of the Holy Spirit, and gifted with the gifts of the Spirit. One of the primary gifts of the Spirit is faith. The Spirit gave Peter and John this gift on the day of the healing.

The gift of faith is available to us, too. It is ours for the ministry we have with people and their needs. It makes us intrepidly daring in calling for Christ's name to be released in the lives of the lame people all around us. By faith we dare to ask that the power of Christ's love, forgiveness, healing, guidance, and hope be infused into the minds, emotions, and bodies of people who desperately need Him.

Power and Blessing for Today

Can miracles like that happen today? It's one thing for Peter and John to heal a lame man. They knew Christ in the flesh; they were fresh from Pentecost. What about us?

The answer to that question can be found in the last section of Peter's sermon in which he clearly declares the messianic age. If people will repent and accept Christ as Messiah, Lord, and Savior, they can participate in God's liberating resources released for them through the Messiah. My understanding of Peter's words is that between the Resurrection and Pentecost and the Second Coming of Christ there will be times of unprecedented blessing through the presence and power of the Lord.

You and I are recipients of this promise. We can realize it through the same response Peter called for from the people of his day: "Repent therefore, and turn again, that your sins may be blotted out." That's what we can do to enter into the messianic age. It means turning from our own devices and resources, confessing our independence and efforts to live on our own strength. Peter promises times of refreshing and restitution, the cool balm of forgiveness and joy, the exchange of our inadequacy for the power of the Lord.

But it means more—a great deal more. The promises to ancient Israel for the messianic age are now given to us, the New Israel. Astounding authority and power are ours. What Paul prayed for the church at Ephesus, I pray for the people of America:

> . . . that the God of our Lord Jesus Christ, the Father of glory, may give you a spirit of wisdom and of revelation as you come to know him, so that, with the eyes of your heart enlightened, you may know what is the hope to which he has called you, what are the riches of his glorious inheritance among the saints, and what is the immeasurable greatness of his power for us who believe, according to the working of his great power. God put this power to work in Christ when he raised him from the dead and seated him at his right hand in the heavenly places, far above all rule and authority and power and dominion, and above every name that is named, not only in this age but also in the age to come. And he has put all things under his feet and has made him the head over all things for the church, which is his body, the fullness of him who fills all in all. (Eph. 1:17-23)

This passage declares what is available to all believers today. We need not wring our hands in frustration. We are not a powerless minority in the face of evil. We can change the course of history, we can alter the trend of evil in our society, we can liberate people if we will pray in the name of Jesus Christ. Prayer is the secret weapon of the Church and Christ's people.

Called to Pray

Once again, focus on the three concerns for anything that has crippled you, the people in your life, or society. How much time have you spent in prayer for these needs? Have you invoked the name of Jesus for the needs of people and society He has placed on your heart?

When Paul wrote instructions to Timothy about how to unlock the incalculable riches of Christ, he said, "First of all, then, I urge that supplications, prayers, intercessions, and thanksgivings be made for everyone, for kings and all who are in high positions, so that we may lead a quiet and peaceable life in all godliness and dignity" (1 Tim. 2:1-2).

The urging admonition is to pray for people. At the top of the list are prayers for people in authority. That means local, state, and national officials. Bad laws and ineffective government are the direct result of inadequate prayer by the people of God. Prayer for the nation in the name of Jesus means prayer for God-appointed people to be elected regardless of party. And it also means that we pray for those who are elected and who hold offices controlling our lives. Good government enables the free preaching of the gospel. We need only to survey history to realize what happens to the Church when freedom of speech and assembly is denied.

We must also confront specific manifestations of evil in society with prayer in Jesus' name. Coupled with that is the Spirit-guided action these prayers clarify. Prayer is itself action, and it can lead to specific steps to implement those prayers. If we were to make a list of officials in government and pray daily for them, I believe we would see results. Each morning I pray for twenty senators and am joined by many who work for the Senate and thousands more across the nation who have joined in a prayer crusade.

If we would make a list of the most crucial problems in our local communities and would unite as congregations to pray, we would not only experience God's intervention, but we would begin to see what we have done to contribute to the evil ourselves, as well as discern practical things our Lord wants us to do.

Challenging Conclusions

This study of Acts 3 has stirred me deeply. I hope nothing less for you. Here are some basic questions that may leave us feeling a bit uncomfortable.

- ◆ The Holy Spirit is moving in a fresh new way in our time. Have I received the Holy Spirit? Is my heart His home?

- ◆ I have been called to be part of the body of Christ. Have I surrendered my separatistic independence to become one in mind and heart with a fellowship of adventurers in the Spirit?
- ◆ Have I recognized and realized the power that is given to me through the Holy Spirit?
- ◆ Have I utilized the power of prayer in Jesus' name for the lameness in myself, in others, and in society?
- ◆ Have I accepted the awesome truth that God will not bypass His people and their prayers and that if I do not pray, His blessings will not be given?

The answers to these questions put me in the place of the paralyzed beggar outside the Beautiful Gate. I have been asking for things, alms of material blessings. The healing and release of a paralyzed spirit, that's what I need! What about you? And when God takes us by the hand and lifts us out of our impotence, then we can see what we must do. Like Peter and John, we must become agents of healing in Jesus' name.

4

From Boredom to Boldness

Counter-Cultural Living

Acts 4

The Library of Congress once sponsored a magnificent exhibit of pictures and artifacts on the development of religion in America. The display began with paintings of scenes of religious persecution in England, Scotland, and on the continent, which prompted the early immigration to America.

I was startled when I saw the first illustration: a drawing of the 1615 Glasgow martyring of John Ogilvie, the only post-Reformation Roman Catholic to be martyred in Scotland. He died a gruesome death. I remembered that John Ogilvie had left the Calvinist persuasion to become a Jesuit priest. There are conflicting stories about the nature of the crime for which he was martyred. Some say he was caught saying the Mass; others indicate that he was punished for treasonous plotting against James VI.

The memory of John Ogilvie is not dead, however. Some years ago, a man by the name of John Fagan was healed of cancer by wearing a medallion of Blessed John Ogilvie. Fagan's wife prayed for

Ogilvie's healing intercession, and her husband was cured. This made Blessed John a candidate for sainthood by the Vatican. After a thorough investigation of his life, miracles, and sacrificial service, he was indeed elevated to sainthood.

About that time, while I was still a pastor in Hollywood, California, a friend of mine sent me a book entitled *Blessed John Ogilvie, Martyred in Scotland* and an article about the canonization. Another friend changed the title of the book cover to read *Lloyd John Ogilvie, Martyred in Hollywood*. We both laughed about that. But then we had a very serious conversation about what *we* would be willing to die for. Saint John Ogilvie had stirred up some challenging reflections.

In America we enjoy spiritual freedom. But what if we lost that blessing and it became a crime to be a Christian? If we were brought to trial, what evidence, material and circumstantial, would the prosecutor be able to use to convict us? Most of us would never be brought to trial, much less convicted, because so little about what we do and say could be identified as Christ's power in us. Why is it that we find it so difficult to talk about what we believe and act on the convictions we hold dearly but never express daringly?

All Christians are called by Christ to express His power and communicate His grace. The Christian life is neither bland nor boring; it's a life of boldness. The blessing of Pentecost was boldness. The early Christians in Acts were marked by the boldness of their Spirit-filled lives.

The Apostles versus the Sanhedrin

In Acts 4, Luke gives us a convicting, convincing comparison of two groups of God's people. Here are two assemblies, the Sanhedrin and the early Church. Both believed they were being faithful and obedient to the truth, but what a contrast.

- One was protective and defensive; the other was powerful and dynamic.
- One believed it had been appointed to conserve the past, keep the peace, and conserve the status quo; the other believed it had been called to communicate the love of God, to witness to a

miraculous intervention of His power, and to live in the resources of His persistent presence.

◆ One was maintained for preservation of rules and regulations;
the other was motivated by an assurance of being right with God.

◆ One was based on what God had given long before; the other
was based on what God was doing right then.

◆ One was symbolized by blandness and boredom; the other by
boldness.

These disturbing questions arise: In which assembly would we be
more comfortable? If you had to identify your church, would it be
more like the Sanhedrin or like the early Church?

Look at how Luke spelled out the contrast. The Sanhedrin was
the highest ruling body of the Jews. It was made up of seventy leaders
plus the high priest, who served as president. In verse 5 of this chapter,
Luke reminds us of the three groups represented in the seventy.
(1) The rulers were the chief priests of the temple. Each was appointed
to represent one of the twenty-four courses or groupings of priests
who served on a weekly rotation in the temple to perform the sacrifices and maintain the purity and propriety of worship. (2) The
elders were the tribal or family heads of the nation. (3) The scribes
were experts in the Law and the oral tradition, the accumulated implications of the Law for practice in daily life.

There were two religious parties represented in the Sanhedrin. One
was the *Pharisees*, many of whom were scribes. They were vigilant,
nationalistic leaders who felt deeply the responsibility for preservation
of the Law, the tradition of the Hebrew people, and the most minute
detail of their religious regulations. They abhorred foreign domination, admitted the possibility of spirits, accepted the idea of resurrection, and awaited the coming of Messiah, but only according to their
carefully defined presuppositions. Most of them had arisen from the
trade class and were known for impeccable legalism.

The *Sadducees* were the landed gentry of the time. They controlled
the wealth, owned most of the land, and wielded immense power.
Collaboration with foreign conquerors was a necessary evil for main-
taining their material position. They wanted peace at any price, and

the price became exorbitantly high under Roman domination. They
wanted no disturbance of the balance of power, the détente they had
carefully worked out with the Roman government. As the wealthy
aristocracy, they held control of the purse strings and kept them
tightly closed around their holdings.

Theologically, the Sadducees were guided by clearly defined convictions that were often in direct opposition to those of the Pharisees.
They did not believe in a resurrection, a life beyond the grave, or
the spirit realm of either angels or devils. They did not anxiously
await, long for, or anticipate the messianic kingdom, for very specific
political reasons. The turbulence and conflict that it would bring
would surely threaten their financial security. Resurrection became
synonymous with revolution. According to scholar F. J. Foakes-
Jackson, "To the Jew of this time, [the resurrection] meant imminent
world catastrophe, in which the powers of the earth would be destroyed and a new order miraculously set up." This would mean
disturbance for those who desperately wanted to keep things as they
were. Now we can see why the Pharisees opposed Jesus and the Sadducees abhorred the early Christians.

Peter and John Arrested

With this adversarial background in mind, we see the plot thicken
in Luke's account of the first trial of the early Christians. The Sad-
ducean party precipitated the conflict. They were enraged at what
the early Church was, did, and believed. The issues were crystal clear:

- They preached the Resurrection.
- They proclaimed a living Lord.
- They lived by a spiritual power through the Holy Spirit.
- They performed miracles that were undeniable proof of their
  power through the Holy Spirit.

After the healing of the lame man at the Beautiful Gate, crowds gath-
ered on Solomon's portico with agitated wonder and amazement.
Peter clearly identified the source of the healing: the name of Jesus
Christ of Nazareth and the release of His power through the Holy

Spirit. Peter forcefully preached that the Christ, whom the Jews had crucified, had been resurrected and was alive, continuing His miraculous ministry through the apostles.

When word of Peter's inflammatory preaching—that "Peter and John were claiming that Jesus had risen from the dead" (Acts 4:2, TLB)—reached the Sadducees, they were "annoyed" and gripped by fear. They quickly gathered the temple police and the chief priests. They could have called the Sanhedrin together, but it was already evening by this time, and Jewish law forbade a trial after sundown. Peter and John were thrown into jail. The Sadducees used the hours of the night to gather their forces so that their party would be represented in a majority, thus tipping the balance of power with the Pharisees when Peter and John came to trial the next morning.

The presentation of the case against the two men the next morning was not easy. The lame man appeared as a material witness to their power. Everyone present was familiar with this beggar who had been lame for forty years. Perhaps many of them had been interrupted on their way to worship by his importuning. That he now was healed and able to stand, walk, and leap, no one could deny.

But it was the quality of boldness in Peter and John that confounded their captors. Amazingly forceful and daring, Peter and John knew what they believed and were able to state it impellingly, using familiar Scriptures and profound theological formulations. Where did they get this boldness? As the Sanhedrin listened, the apostles' words were painfully familiar. They had heard them before! They sounded like Jesus of Nazareth, whom this very court had tried illegally in the dark of night. Perhaps both Peter and John were on criminal "wanted lists" because of their devoted discipleship to the Nazarene rabbi whom these leaders thought they had destroyed forever.

But Peter and John were so convincingly articulate. Where did this eloquence, which in some ways exceeded the most learned expression, come from? They were untrained fishermen, without authorized theological education. No doubt about it—they were recognized as "companions of Jesus" (vs. 13). The grammar of the Sanhedrin's surmise is telling. They simply asserted that Peter and John had been followers of Jesus in His earthly ministry. Little did they comprehend that the apostles had been with Him the day before the lame man's healing and that the resurrected Lord was with them right then!

On Trial

There had to be some way to trap these Christians, to establish some charge. The Sadducees among the Sanhedrin led the cross-examination, longing to establish evidence that would convince their fellow party members that Peter and John were worthy of condemnation or death. Deuteronomy 13:1-5 was used as the basis of the trial:

> If prophets or those who divine by dreams appear among you and promise you omens or portents, and the omens or the portents declared by them take place, and they say, "Let us follow other gods" (whom you have not known) "and let us serve them," you must not heed the words of those prophets or those who divine by dreams; for the LORD your God is testing you, to know whether you indeed love the LORD your God with all your heart and soul. . . . But those prophets or those who divine by dreams shall be put to death for having spoken treason against the LORD your God. . . . So you shall purge the evil from your midst.

The idea was that anyone performing a sign had to prove that it was from God and that they used it to honor and glorify Him and to lead people closer to Him. That's exactly where the Sadducees failed. Peter and John had done both. They gave God the glory and called the people to praise Him for it.

The hands of the Sanhedrin were tied. The undeniable evidence of an authentic miracle stood before them—the lame man, well and irrefutably energetic. All they could do was warn Peter and John and charge them never again to speak in or of the name of Jesus. What a futile attempt! It was like trying to reverse the direction of a fast-moving stream or hold back the undauntable winds of a hurricane. What a pitiful plea they made:

> What shall we do with these men? We can't deny that they have done a tremendous miracle, and everybody in Jerusalem knows

about it. But perhaps we can stop them from spreading their propaganda. We'll tell them that if they do it again, we'll really throw the book at them. (Acts 4:16-17, TLB)

The threats they leveled at Peter and John were to no avail. Their answer was powerful: "You decide whether God wants us to obey you instead of him! We cannot stop telling about the wonderful things we saw Jesus do and heard him say" (vss. 19-20, TLB). What could the Sanhedrin do with that? If they punished Peter and John, it would start a riot among the people who favored the apostles. Everyone was praising God for the miraculous healing of the lame man. The Sanhedrin released the two men, hoping against hope that it would be the last time they would see or hear anything of them.

The Source of Boldness

Afterwards Peter and John returned to the fellowship of the local church and gathered together to pray. Note the content of their supplication—they prayed for boldness! In the prayers of the early Church we find the explanation for Peter and John's boldness during their arrest and trial. Let us consider first the substance of their boldness and then evaluate its source in the prayers of the Church.

The word *boldness* means "lucid and daring statement." In the Greek the word is *parrēsia*, "telling it all" (*pan rēsis*). It entails both conviction and enunciation of undeniable truths. There could be no mistaking the meaning. Boldness is a blunt, almost blatant and defiant enunciation that commands attention. There is no apology, no faltering, but a "thus saith the Lord" clarity. The apostles brandished a sanctified stubbornness. Their hearts were possessed by a great affection, and their minds were directed by a clear purpose declared with liberating freshness. Boldness is rooted in truth, expressed in daily witness, and acted out in undeniable evidence of its implications.

When we review Acts 4, we see the motives for and the nature of Peter and John's boldness. First, the Resurrection, this essential miracle of God, *made courageous people out of cowards.* If death was not an ending but only a transition in living, they could face anything and endure everything. Christ's death and Resurrection set them free to live with joy. His words were the drumbeat in their hearts: "I am the resurrection and the life; those who believe in me, even though they die, will live, and everyone who lives and believes in me will never die" (John 11:25-26). Resurrection and life—the two must be kept together. The fact that Christ arose is one thing, but that He is still with us is something even greater.

The second reason for the remarkable lives of the apostles was *their experience of the risen Christ.* Because Jesus was alive, they could face all of life's limitations. It was by the power and authority of His name that they feared no one and no thing. Peter said, "It is by his authority that this man stands here healed!" (Acts 4:10, TLB).

The third reason for the apostles' boldness was *the tangible miracle of healing that had been performed.* Peter and John realized that the power of the living Christ was at work through them. The actual manifestation of healing quickened their faith.

The fourth source of strength for Peter and John was the *objective standard of Scripture.* In his speech Peter quoted Psalm 118:22, "The stone that the builders rejected has become the chief cornerstone" and Isaiah 28:16, "Therefore thus says the Lord GOD, See, I am laying in Zion a foundation stone, a tested stone, a precious cornerstone, a sure foundation." Jesus was the fulfillment of the prophets of old. He was the foundation stone or the keystone at the top of a corner, binding the walls together where they meet. Perhaps Peter meant both ideas. The point is that when we are founded on Scripture, on something more than our own subjective ideas and feelings, we are able to move forward with unlimited audacity. Added to the Old Testament Scriptures, the objective standard for these apostles was the life and message of Jesus. They knew what to do and what to say because they remembered what He had done and said.

The fifth reason for their confidence was that *they were filled with the Holy Spirit.* Note in Luke's account that there is a difference between being "full of the Holy Spirit" and being "filled with the Holy Spirit." The first begins when we surrender our lives and open ourselves to be containers and transmitters of the living Spirit of God. The second materializes for special needs and opportunities in ministry and for witnessing to the world.

In verse 8 Luke tells us that Peter was "filled." The past aorist passive participle *plētheis*, "filled," indicates an act performed upon Peter rather than a continuing state. It also refers to a promise Jesus had made earlier to His disciples: "When they bring you before the synagogues, the rulers, and the authorities, do not worry about how you are to defend yourselves or what you are to say; for the Holy Spirit will teach you at that very hour what you ought to say" (Luke 12:11-12). The crucial truth to remember is that the Holy Spirit is both Sanctifier and Source of special strength. It is by the Spirit's gift of faith that we believe. It is through the influence of the Spirit that we grow in assurance and Christlike character. But it is also through a special outpouring that we become equipped for unique situations, problems, challenges, or crises.

The worst that can happen to us always brings about the best that the Spirit has to give us. When Peter was "filled with the Holy Spirit," the Spirit took possession of his mind, saturated his emotions, compelled his will, and pulsated through his body. That's why Peter and the early Church had boldness! In his book *Earliest Christianity: A.D. 30-150*, Johannes Weiss observed that the early Christians had "a tempestuous enthusiasm, an overwhelming intensity of feeling, an immediate awareness of the presence of God, an inconquerable sense of power, and an irresistible control over the will and inner spirit and even the physical conditions of other men—these are the ineradicable features of historic early Christianity."

The sixth reason for the boldness of the early Christians was not just that Jesus saves, but that *only Jesus saves.* An exclusion led to a bold inclusiveness. When we believe that our Lord is not just the best of good men, or one Savior among many, we are filled with an urgency that expresses itself in boldness.

The various translations of Acts 4:12 are helpful and compelling. The Moffatt version says, "There is no salvation by anyone else, nor even a second name under heaven appointed for us men and our salvation." *The Living Bible* renders it: "There is salvation in no one else! Under all heaven there is no other name for men to call upon to save them." The key word is *salvation,* which actually means healing and health, wholeness and oneness. Through the Cross of Christ and His indwelling power we are reconciled to God, renewed in self-acceptance, released from guilt and self-justification, reunited with others in accepting love, and reconstituted as agents of hope in the world. No religion or cult can promise that!

The Secret of Strength

Now we can understand boldness: it is clear vision, absolute certainty, strong conviction, and unflinching courage. Contemporary Christians and the Church of our time have no greater need. How shall we find it? The prayers of the early Church at the conclusion of chapter 4 give us the secret of their source of strength.

What an amazing response the Church gave to Peter and John's report—not fear nor wavering trepidation, but prayer. We need to consider this prayer as a model, for it gives an outline of how they sustained their boldness. Note the convictions that saturated the prayer and supplication.

The undergirding conviction is of the absolute sovereignty of God over all life: "Sovereign Lord, who made the heaven and the earth, the sea, and everything in them," they prayed. The word for *Lord* here is different from the one used elsewhere in the New Testament. In this case it is *despota,* meaning "despot," or in its deeper implication, "absolute ruler, final sovereign, master." There was no doubt in the early Church that the Lord was in charge of all things.

Coupled closely with this faith was the assurance that only the Lord was worthy of trust. They had learned that their hope was not in people. They had also learned that they were in good company. The painful difficulties they were facing were not unlike what happened to David, who had written about the same problems centuries before: "The kings of the earth took their stand, and the rulers have gathered together against the Lord and against his Messiah" (Ps. 2:2). It's a great comfort to know that God's faithful people have always been in trouble. In fact, it's often a sign that we are obeying God rather than people. So what's new about persecution for righteousness' sake? Jesus called it blessed.

We can deal with persecution if we're sure of the next thing the Church asserted: God's overruling power. God allowed the Cross, but He had the final word in the Resurrection. So the Church could pray, "For in this city, in fact, both Herod and Pontius Pilate, with the Gentiles and the people of Israel, gathered together against your holy servant Jesus, whom you anointed, to do whatever your hand and your plan had predestined to take place" (vss. 27-28).

Jesus was not a helpless victim. God was in Christ there on Calvary. What the people in power thought was the worst they could do to get rid of Jesus was used for the best that God could give, because He would never rid Himself of human beings and their needs. God can use anything that happens to us. He constantly brings good out of evil or difficulty. Nothing is meaningless. We can never drift beyond His overruling intervention and ultimate plan.

Those convictions are now expressed in confidence: "And now, Lord, look at their threats, and grant to your servants to speak your word with all boldness." They ask for more of the very thing that had gotten them into trouble in the first place. Amazing! But note the reason in verse 30: "while you stretch out your hand to heal." They were asking God to continue the healings that had caused such consternation. They knew all power in heaven and earth was theirs through the name of Jesus. Nothing could stop the movement now. "And signs and wonders are performed through the name of your holy servant Jesus." What a conclusion to a daring prayer. The spectacular events spread across the pages of Acts must all be traced back to praying like that.

The Lord's answer to the prayer came when the room where they were assembled shook, "and they were all filled with the Holy Spirit and spoke the word of God with boldness." Again Luke uses the word *filled,* this time in a tense that indicates a special filling occurred. Inflow and outgo were in direct proportion. They were especially equipped for the particular task at hand and spoke out boldly.

Boldness for Today

Where do you need the gift of boldness today and through this next week? Can you picture yourself as God's bold person in that situation or with that person? How would you act? What would you say?

What would you dare? Perhaps it's a word, or an act of love, or a witness for the Lord you have been reluctant to make because of fear or embarrassment or timidity. Perhaps the bold act is one of reconciliation or restitution that must be performed at great cost of pride or prejudice. Maybe it's taking a stand for what you believe at home or at work or among people whose approval you desperately need. It may be stepping out in faith to confront some social evil even at the loss of financial comfort or security.

Whatever the situation, picture it vividly. Then ask for a special filling of the Holy Spirit. He is undeniably faithful. He will give us power to act and speak with boldness, and life will become thrilling again—be sure of that.

5
A Life That Demands Explanation

Acts 5:17-42

I t's interesting how advertisers and opportunists of all kinds use the idea of the "good life" to sell everything from beer to suburban living. They know how to touch the raw nerve in all of us. In one week I found 360 uses of the word *life* in advertisements. We all join the chorus and sing the lusty words with gusto, "I love life and I want to live!"

But what is life and what does it mean to live it to the fullest? Some of us have been given the privilege of tasting and touching all that we are told will bring happy living and have found the promises oversold. No place, position, personality, prowess, prosperity, or relationship is able to pull it off for us. We still long for something more.

The quest for life is not new. It has been aching in the heart of humanity for a long time. It was the foundation of the voracious spiritual hunger of people in Jerusalem when the first Church was born. Their eager response to the early Christians was based on the fact that they modeled a quality of life that was attractive, magnetic, and powerful. People who heard them talk about their new life in

Christ, empowered by the Holy Spirit, wanted what these Christians had. Their vibrancy, their love and acceptance of each other, and their indomitable vision and purpose created a hunger in people to taste the same quality of life.

The life they were living with the resurrected Christ and with each other demanded an explanation and a response. And what a response! Believers flocked to the church; healing power was unleashed; and Jerusalem was shaken by a pervading spiritual revival.

We are told that the Church became of "one heart and soul" (Acts 4:32), and gave sacrificially to everyone who had need. Powerful signs and wonders were performed daily in the temple in Solomon's portico. People came from everywhere to be healed. Finally, in Acts 5, the ruling Jewish leaders had enough and once again arrested the apostles.

New Life with a Mission

I believe that Peter and John were thrown into prison not just for the message they preached, but also for the magnificent life they were living. Acts 5:17 tells us that the Sadducees were jealous and angry. They had sternly warned the apostles to speak no more in the name of Jesus, and the apostles had disobeyed. The Sanhedrin thought there was nothing left to do but lock up the apostles. But they could not lock up the truth they proclaimed nor the Lord they obeyed. The proud Sadducees miscalculated the power of both.

Late at night an angel of the Lord opened the prison doors and brought out the apostles. An angel is a messenger, an emissary of the Lord sent to accomplish a particular task. Astounding as those unlocked doors were to the Christians, what this angel *said* was more important than what he did. The angel's words confirmed what the apostles had been doing and challenged them to continue without reservation. It must have been a stirring moment: a clear word of direction from the Lord. They had been on the right track; now they were to move ahead with all stops pulled out. The Lord knew the need for life in people's hearts.

It is not surprising, then, that the angel's admonition was a propitious, emboldening call and recall to the central message and mission of the Church. Here was an unpolished, unambiguous directive leaving no doubt about what the apostles should do and say, and it has stood as the undeniable purpose of Christians and the Church ever since. If we want an objective standard by which to measure our lives or the effectiveness of our churches, it is here in the angel's mobilizing commission: "Go and stand in the temple and speak to the people all the words of this Life" (Acts 5:20, RSV). Note the capital *L* in Life. The apostles were to speak not just about life, but about this new *Life* in particular.

The King James Version states it as, "Go stand and speak in the temple to the people all the words of this life." *The New English Bible* translates the heartening words, "Speak to the people about this new life and all that it means." The Phillips is even more straightforward, catching the urgency and inclusiveness: "Go and . . . tell the people all about this new life." Here were marching orders to go offer the grandest gift the Lord had to give for the greatest need the people had. Go take your stand. Tell people about Life. Don't leave anything out. Tell them all about it!

What Is This New Life in Christ?

The word *life* is used thirty-six times in the New Testament in reference to Christ and the dimension of living He revealed. We need to recapture that power-packed meaning if we are to do what the apostles did. We have been unlocked from our own prisons of fear, inhibition, ambiguity, and confusion. Like the apostles, we too have been delivered to declare and dramatize life. Let's look at several aspects of this life in Christ.

1. Life is a synonym for the Lord himself.
This new life begins with Jesus: "In him was life, and the life was the light of all people" (John 1:4). The witness of the early Church was clear:

> We declare to you what was from the beginning, what we have heard, what we have seen with our eyes, what we have looked at and touched with our hands, concerning the word of life—this life was revealed, and we have seen it and testify to it, and declare to

you the eternal life that was with the Father and was revealed to us. (1 John 1:1-2)

There was no other adequate way to put it: Jesus was life—God's life incarnate and the picture of what He intended life to be. In Christ we see what God is like and what we are to become.

2. Life is the synthesis of what Jesus came to be and do.
There are three self-disclosing "I am" statements in which Jesus declared Himself as the Life. "I am the bread of life" (John 6:35)—the essential basis of nurture and sustenance. "I am the resurrection and the life" (John 11:25)—through His Resurrection we are given the quality of eternal life. "I am the way, and the truth, and the life" (John 14:6)—the way to fellowship with God, the truth about God and His nature, and the life of God in history and in the mind and heart of a believer.

All of this is summed up in Jesus' own delineation of His purpose: "I came that they may have life, and have it abundantly" (John 10:10). The abundant life encompasses a new level of existence. Beyond plant, animal, and human levels of life, there is a totally new dimension of creation. It is life lived by His limitless power, guided by His love, expressed by His grace, and totally indestructible by death. Paul expressed this triumphant truth to the Corinthians: "So if anyone is in Christ, there is a new creation: everything old has passed away; see, everything has become new!" (2 Cor. 5:17)

3. Life is symbolic of what happens to a person in relationship to Christ.
Jesus was incarnated life and now He imparts that life to those who will receive Him. Jesus promised that He would make His home in us. Paul put it plainly, "Christ in you, the hope of glory" (Col. 1:27). The early Church father Irenaeus agreed, stating, "The glory of God is a man fully alive." Paul explained to the Galatians how this full life happened to him: "I have been crucified with Christ; it is no longer I who live, but it is Christ who lives in me. And the life I now live in the flesh I live by faith in the Son of God, who loved me and gave himself for me" (Gal. 2:20). For Paul, Christ was the source of this new life.

The apostle John gives us a blunt conclusion to the symbol of life as the description of what happens to us: "Whoever has the Son has life; whoever does not have the Son of God does not have life" (1 John 5:12). John Henry Newman leaves us with the same unsettling truth. "Fear not that your life will come to an end, but rather that it shall never have a beginning." The cycle of death and resurrection is the key. We die to our willful control of our lives and we are resurrected to new life as Christ lives His life through us. It doesn't matter how long we live but whether we find Life in the midst of living.

4. Life is the balanced symmetry of relationships.
We often speak of the "life" of a church or the "life" that Christians share together. Part of the proclamation of the Christian life is the miracle of fellowship, unity, and oneness. Since most people's problems appear in their relationships, often the most forceful aspect of presenting the gospel is sharing with people what happens when Christ's grace becomes the basic ingredient of our attitudes and dispositions.

There can be no question that the effectiveness of the early Church in evangelism was caused by the love shared by the Christians. "How those Christians love one another!" was the world's telling response. Jesus promised that "by this everyone will know that you are my disciples, if you have love for one another" (John 13:35). Christ's life in a believer brings a totally different quality to that believer's bond with fellow believers. Christ's love, forgiveness, esteem, and hope become the basis of each relationship.

At the close of the senators' Bible study, often we go around the circle giving each senator a chance to share a personal need. Then we go back around as each person prays for the needs of the person on his or her right. One day as we did this, I was amazed at the unity between senators across party and ideological lines. As they experienced the Life, they were encouraging each other to discover the exciting adventure of life in Christ.

Living It Out
The four aspects of life in Christ are focused in the angel's instruction to Christians to stand in the temple and tell the message. The dimen-

sions of that message are expanded by the phrase, "all the words" of this life. "Don't leave anything out," the challenge implies. "Tell the people *all* you know about life."

That's what we need to hear and obey in our "go for the gusto" world. Our task is not to argue, philosophize, speculate, or cajole, but to live a life that demands explanation. Is there anything about us that would force people to say, "That's the way I wish I could live." When we consider sharing our faith as actually imparting *life*, what a difference it makes! Then the emphasis is on Christ and not on theories about Him that we try to force upon people.

"All the words of this life" must become our own experience. Christ must become our life, our consuming passion, purpose, and power. This means spending time with Him in prayer so that He can reshape our personalities around His own. It means continually renewing our experience of life in Him by allowing Him to guide our decisions, attitudes, words, and expression. And it also means grasping with daily freshness the meaning His death and Resurrection have for our problems and concerns. In this way we will live a life that demands explanation.

The apostles' mysterious release and subsequent appearance in the temple demanded an explanation. Luke, breaking into the intensity of his biography of the Acts of the Holy Spirit, presents the consternation of the Sanhedrin in comic relief.

Imagine the scene: The Sanhedrin were gathered in glorious array ready to sentence the apostles. Officers were sent to bring the apostles before them. We can feel the frustration they experienced as the report came back that the prison was still securely locked but the apostles were not there! While they discussed this with befuddled alarm, an even more unsettling report came: "Look, the men you put in prison are standing in the temple and teaching the people!" How could the Sadducees explain that away? They did not accept the existence of spirits or interceding influence from God. How did those apostles get free? There was nothing left to do but arrest them again and proceed with the trial.

This has penetrating meaning for us. If we are to live a life in Christ that demands explanation, it's not only the observable quality of our lives that is important, but also evidence that shows there is a power at work in us. People must be forced to wonder and see that there is more than personality prowess or healthy maturity at work. They must come to know that there is something—Someone—more than ourselves enabling us to live the life that attracts attention.

It's how we live through life's pressures and potentials that makes people wonder what hidden inner resource has released us from the prisons of life. People should be saying, "He could never have done that on his own strength!" or, "Where does she get the patience and love she always seems to have regardless of what happens or what people say?" or, "What is it about him that frees him from the hang-ups that keep me stuck in compulsive patterns?"

A man once told me about the influence a Christian friend had on him:

> I watched him for months. It was not so much what he said. Neither was it the way he reacted in crises, though he is consistently strong and calm. No, it's the way I feel when I'm with him. He makes me feel of value, like I am the only person alive when he talks to me. He is so free! Finally, late one evening at a party, I got him in a corner and asked, "How did you find what you've got?" Then he told me about Christ in the most unreligious, non-pious way I've ever heard. We've talked a lot since then. I can now say that I'm a Christian. Some church people really turn me off, but this guy is irresistible!

That should be happening to all of us constantly in our relationships. Our task is to know Christ so well and to grow so deeply in Him that we don't have to sit around worrying about how to witness. If we allow our Lord to live in us and spend our energies cultivating friendship with Him, we will become witnesses. Be sure of that! The Lord Himself will position people in our lives because He knows we're ready.

Results of Release from Our Prisons
Most of us find sharing our faith a bit difficult. Someone once asked,

"Why is it that so few Christians talk about what's happening to
them in their faith?" The pointed reply was, "Maybe it's because there
is so little that's happening!" I suggest that we need the same reorienting challenge that was given to the apostles and a release from the
prisons of the past or present to back it up. The two must always
be kept together: the Lord's clear word and undeniable evidence in
our lives of an opened prison door.

Look at the results in the apostles' lives as they are brought before
the Sanhedrin and are pressed again to explain why they persisted in
following and proclaiming Christ.

There is *courage:* "We must obey God rather than any human
authority." The same goes for us. We cannot speak "all the words of
this new life" until we are free from all secondary loyalties and securities of the old life. It is relevant to us that Peter rose above the
entangling web of dependence upon approval and safety. Then he
could speak a decisive word to people bound up in the constricting
chains of tradition and cultural religion. What a tragedy it is when
our need for acceptance by people who do not know Christ is so
strong that we cannot dare to live and share the only hope that can
set them free. How many Christians can say, "We must obey God
rather than people"? Can I say that? Can you?

There is *clarity:* Peter once again enunciated the essential elements
of the gospel. Fearlessly he said, "We are witnesses!" But not to himself or his accomplishment—he witnessed to Christ! He used two
words to describe Christ: "Leader and Savior" (vs. 31). The word
leader is the same Greek word Peter used before in Acts 3:15, translated as "Author of life." Here it has a different feel and intention.
It comes from the Greek word *archēgos* (translated as "pioneer" in
Hebrews 12:2) and is closely related to an Aramaic term for a strong
swimmer, often a part of a crew on a vessel. If anything happened
to a ship and the turbulent sea prevented getting through the rocks
and reefs to shore, this member of the crew would tie a rope around
his waist, dive into the angry sea, and swim ashore. After firmly
attaching the rope on shore, he would assist the others as they followed the rope to safety. Christ was that kind of lifesaver for Peter.
The Savior for all humankind now helped Peter, the big fisherman,

to safety. That's why he could talk so forcefully about repentance and forgiveness.

Then there is *confidence:* The interceding angel and the persistent presence of the Holy Spirit assured Peter that the apostles were not alone. The living Christ was the unseen but strongly felt witness. No wonder Peter could say, "And we are witnesses to these things, and so is the Holy Spirit whom God has given to those who obey him" (vs. 32). There's nothing we can't attempt, no needed witness we should fear to give, if we are backed up by the living God Himself!

Last, there is a *condition:* Peter clearly says the Holy Spirit is given to "those who obey." Obedience is the secret to spiritual strength. We must obey what Christ says in His message; we must obey what comes to us from reading His Word; and we must obey the deep inner voice of His guidance for particular situations and relationships. How do you know if you're being obedient? I find it helpful to ask myself the following questions:

- ◆ Am I living consistently as much of Christ as I know?
- ◆ Am I living out the implications of what I discover daily in the Scriptures?
- ◆ Do I refuse to do what is necessary to be faithful to Christ? Has He already told me more than I have acted on?
- ◆ Am I consciously inhibited from speaking about my Lord because of fear of rejection or of being considered foolish, unintellectual, or uncultured?

The power of the Holy Spirit is released by obedience. There is no other way. We cannot expect the joy and energy of His infilling if we are saying no to what we know we should do. Obedience is like a thermostat. It opens the flow of the Spirit for the needs around us. The cold world demands the heat and warmth of the Holy Spirit's fire within us.

Unexplainable Joy

One last thing needs to be said about this passage. We have seen what obedience to the angel's admonition did for the multitudes in Jerusalem. Now observe and feel what it did for the Church itself. After the apostles were beaten and charged, they left the council and "rejoiced that they were considered worthy to suffer dishonor for the sake of the name" (vs. 41). *The Amplified Bible* says they were "dignified by the indignity." They rejoiced because they had been faithful. The flush of delight in God and one's self after a time of obedience seems to be the Lord's way of saying, "Well done, good and faithful servant."

Joy is the undeniable mark of the new life. We are not expected to be perfect, or never fail, or be free of life's pressuring problems. But joy is the identifiable evidence that Christ is alive in us and we are facing reality with His guidance, interceptions, and undiminishable strength. It's a joy that no circumstance or situation can produce. A joy-filled life will always demand explanation. And we will be ready. We have been released from the prison of a life that is not life at all, to live a new life in Christ and to spread the news to those whom God has ready to listen.

6

The Power of One

The Cost of Being a Witness

Acts 6:1–8:3

I once attended a showing of several precious art objects to be auctioned off to the highest bidder. One famous painting had been advertised and used as an enticement to attract people to come. However, when I saw it, there was a sign beneath the painting saying "Not for sale, at any price." An experienced buyer stood beside me admiring the painting, but was not impressed by the exclusive sign. "Ha! Everything has a price," he said. "It just takes time and a lot of money."

As I reflected on his statement, I wondered if his observation was true for people too. Does everyone have a price—that point where convictions, concerns, and commitment become secondary? In Acts 6 and 7, we discover one man who was not for sale at any price. We also find out how powerful one person's faithful witness can be.

Luke brings Stephen to center stage in his drama of the acts of the Holy Spirit. The scene is brief, but the results of what Stephen did and said are eternal. It would not be an exaggeration to say that if Stephen had not played his part well, with obedience and faithfulness, Luke would have had little more to record than a tale about an innocuous sect of Judaism that didn't last long enough to be given a name. Without Stephen there might not have been a break with Judaism, a world expansion of the Church, an apostle Paul, or a faith vital enough that the followers of Jesus would eventually be called, with a mixture of admiration and rage, "the Christians." In fact, if it hadn't been for Stephen, I probably would not be writing this, and chances are that you would have little desire to read it.

Problems in the Growing Church

Luke prepares his readers carefully for Stephen's entrance by describing a problem in the Church that had to be handled with discernment. Two distinct types of Jews responded to the forceful proclamation of the gospel by the apostles in those early days of the Church. There were the Palestinian Jews, *the Hebrews* (Acts 6:1) who were descendants of those brought back to Jerusalem by Nehemiah and Ezra after the Dispersion. They spoke either Hebrew or Aramaic and were proud of their exclusive and impeccable observance of their undefiled tradition. Then there were the Grecian Jews, or *the Hellenists,* who had descended from those who had been victims of the Dispersion under the captivity of Babylon centuries before. Their numbers were swelled by others who had been drawn away from Palestine by economic and business pursuits.

Though they had settled throughout the Mediterranean world and beyond, the Hellenists never lost their love for Jerusalem and the temple. They shared the passion of the motto of Jews through the ages to return to Jerusalem, "Next year in Jerusalem!" Often these Hellenist Jews, who spoke Greek and were ingrained with Greek culture, would remain in Jerusalem after a pilgrimage to the Holy City. But they were never fully accepted as equals by the Palestinian Jews.

This long-standing tension was healed among the Jews of both groups who became new people in Christ and shared the love of the Church's fellowship. Well, almost! Acts 6:1 says that some of the Hellenists complained that their widows were being slighted in the distribution of the shared benevolence from the fellowship. The offerings of the believers were given to the apostles for allocation to those in need. Somehow, the Hellenists felt their widows were not being given a fair share and that the Hebrews were being given a preference—a little problem that forced the apostles to face a big concern.

As the Church grew into the thousands, the apostles were spending all their time with administrative problems and had little time for preaching the gospel. This seemingly insignificant frustration led to a very significant solution. They recommended that the Church elect seven men of good standing to "wait on tables" (6:2). By that they meant more than what a waiter does at a restaurant today. A *table* at that time meant a place where a money-changer collected or exchanged money. The deacons were elected to oversee the distribution of the monies and provisions to the needy among the fellowship. And all of those elected were Hellenistic Jews. Little did they know that their contention would bring about the election and ordination of a Hellenic Jew who would change the course of history.

A Man Full of the Holy Spirit

Long before we witness the flow from the watershed event of Stephen's life, Luke paints a word portrait of how the Lord made Stephen a man of integrity and conviction.

We are told that Stephen was "full of faith and the Holy Spirit" (6:5). The two dimensions belong inseparably together. The greatest gift of the Holy Spirit is faith. It is the gift that makes all other gifts possible. This gift not only liberates a person to respond to the gospel, but frees him or her to dare to believe that all things are possible through Christ. Faith first produces the new life in Christ and then a new life of daring in the believer. The Holy Spirit gave Stephen the courage to surrender his life to Christ and then to anticipate expectantly Christ's intervention in all situations. The power of faith produced a viable relationship between Stephen and the living Christ. Whatever else we admire about this fearless saint, we find the ultimate taproot of our admiration in his audacious faith.

Next, we are told that Stephen was "full of grace and power" (6:8). The word *grace* has tremendous implications here. Stephen had been healed by Christ's unlimited, unmerited, unearnable love. He was a released man. Defensiveness, self-justification, and competitiveness disappeared. Graciousness became the discernible trait of his personality. He took on the disposition of Christ. Faith got him started, grace kept him growing, and spiritual power was the result.

Our world has tarnished the meaning of a "powerful person." For Luke it meant that Stephen had the capacity to communicate the gospel well, the liberty to lead people into a relationship with the Savior effectively, and the power to bring healing and hope to physically and mentally depleted people. Stephen was a rare combination of administrator, preacher, and teacher. But the administrative position to which the Church ordained him only served as the Lord's launching pad for lifting him into the orbit of teaching and preaching in his own synagogue in Jerusalem.

Fortified by the signs and wonders that put an exclamation point behind everything he said, Stephen went to the synagogue of the Freedmen to preach the gospel. This synagogue was the special place of worship and fellowship for Hellenistic Jews in Jerusalem. Its membership was made up of Jews from Alexandria, Cyrenia, Cilicia, and the Roman province of Asia. It was customary in that synagogue to raise and debate religious issues. The Jews who listened to Stephen had not anticipated being captivated by his persuasive rhetoric and message. In their response, we learn more—a great deal more—about Stephen's Christ-centered character: "They could not withstand the wisdom and the Spirit with which he spoke." Again we encounter an aspect of his charismatic, that is, grace-gifted, life.

Stephen had the gift of wisdom. That means the indwelling Spirit gave him great understanding and insight, coupled with discernment. He could understand the deep mysteries of God's nature and His purposes for His people. The Spirit gave Stephen thoughts beyond his innate intellectual capacity and lucidness beyond his learning. The Greek-oriented and trained Jews were startled and amazed at his wise and penetrating presentation. No wonder they could not withstand it! It was the Spirit of God speaking through him.

Don't miss the progression through which Luke has taken us in his character study of Stephen. The Holy Spirit was alive and at work in Stephen. That gave him the gift of faith to appropriate the gospel and accept Jesus as Lord. This conviction produced his character. He became a grace-oriented, gracious man in Christ, which gave him the power to implement Christ's will in the world around him. Wonders and signs resulted. What he subsequently taught and preached was impelling and irrefutable. He could not be dissuaded or bought off. Nothing the leaders of the synagogue could do or say diminished his determination or muddled his clarity.

A Man with a Mission

Among the Cilicians in the synagogue was a brilliant Pharisee from Tarsus, the principal city of Cilicia. He had been brought back to Jerusalem by the Sanhedrin to spearhead an attack on the indomitable and troublesome followers of Jesus. Trained under Gamaliel and one of the master teacher's most brilliant students, he now listened with rage to Stephen's declaration that the crucified Jesus of Nazareth was the Messiah. The Pharisee's name was Saul of Tarsus.

My supposition is that Saul was a member of the synagogue of the Freedmen (where Stephen preached) and was at this time already engaged in his assignment to destroy the Church. He was probably among those who were drawn in by the deacon's wisdom and spirit. Nothing enrages an arrogant intellectual more than to be defeated in the arena of his or her expertise. Saul was a determined man who did not want to be embarrassed before his own synagogue.

Saul versus Stephen. Human intellect and brilliance pitted against Holy Spirit-inspired wisdom and knowledge. Both Hellenistic Jews, each had a passion he could not sublimate nor subdue. It is my belief that Saul was the mastermind behind the scheme to destroy Stephen. He had to find a way. He recruited people to lie and say that Stephen blasphemed the temple and contradicted the commandments of Moses. The trumped-up charge was carefully worded when Stephen was brought before the council. The Sanhedrin stated: "This man never stops saying things against this holy place and the law; for we have heard him say that this Jesus of Nazareth will destroy this place and will change the customs that Moses handed on to us" (6:13-14).

It was an old charge, not unlike the one leveled at Jesus himself. But it was very accurate and very false at the same time: Stephen did not cease to speak, that's true; but he did not speak against the holy place or the law, he simply spoke *for* Jesus and a new life in Him as Messiah. He did not claim that Jesus would destroy the temple, but that God was greater than any place built by people. He did say that Jesus enabled a new quality of relationship with God by repentance and forgiveness, which would supersede old, worn-out practices of human-made religion.

The Sanhedrin could not understand a man like Stephen. He could not be threatened, bought off, or punished into subservience. All they could do was listen and look "intently at him, and they saw that his face was like the face of an angel" (6:15).

There's the capping phrase of our character study. What did the Sanhedrin know about angels? Think how the expression on Stephen's face must have affected these ecclesiastics. Resoluteness, determination, vision, brightness more than human brilliance shone through those piercing eyes, coupled with warmth, love, and irresistible entreaty. Stephen's angelic face would not allow their eyes to turn away. All that we have learned about the characteristics of Stephen's charisma is focused on his face.

The people around us can always read our hearts by our faces. The inner things we live with will show upon our faces. The soul is dyed with the color of its commitment. What happens to a person's face when the light in his or her heart goes out or no flame has ever been set to blaze? Our countenance is connected to our character and our character to our communion with the living God. No palm-reading medium is necessary to know someone. Look at his or her face!

Stephen's Defense

What Saul saw on Stephen's face that day never reached his heart. Saul's commission to destroy the followers of the Nazarene had been awarded because of his vigilant commitment to the law and strict observance of the customs of Israel. Like a lawyer trying his first case, Saul was determined to win at all costs. He would not be dissuaded, however brilliant was Stephen's face or rhetoric. If he could expose Stephen for blasphemy and do it according to Deuteronomic law, he would have a precedent for the subsequent destruction of the sect.

Deuteronomy 17:2-7 fit his strategy perfectly. Stephen had, in Saul's judgment, transgressed the covenant and was serving another god, this Jesus of Nazareth. The Pharisee of Tarsus was already gathering authentic witnesses to enact Moses' prescribed punishment. Stephen's death by stoning was sealed in Saul's heart.

He must have been a bit impatient when the chief priest asked for Stephen's defense of himself in Acts 7. Stephen's magnificent review of Israel's history in the light of Jesus as the Messiah must have impressed Saul's mind, steeped as he was in Israel's history and disciplined by Greek learning. He must have admired the breadth of Stephen's knowledge of Scripture. But truth can be inflammatory to a person set on a determined course. Saul was probably not only attracted but repelled as Stephen got too close to his raw nerve.

When Stephen declared with prophetic power that the leaders of Israel to whom he spoke were "stiff-necked people, uncircumcised in heart and ears, you are forever opposing the Holy Spirit" (7:51), Saul knew that Stephen had written his own death warrant. Now Saul could step back and let the dam break and allow the polluted waters of hatred to inundate Stephen. The Sadducees and Pharisees of the high court were so enraged that they ground their teeth against him. Like a pack of ravenous wolves, they gnashed their fangs, ready.

Stephen felt the danger, the overwhelming hatred. What could he do now? Nothing other than what he had done all through his brief new life in the Savior. He called for help! He looked up and knew that the Lord was with him: "But filled with the Holy Spirit, he gazed into heaven and saw the glory of God and Jesus standing at the right hand of God." What else can that mean than that his eyes of faith, strengthened by the Holy Spirit, had a vision of the power of God focused on the Lord Jesus? He was not alone. The Lord was faithful to His promise. In a triumphant affirmation of faith Stephen cried out, "Look, I see the heavens opened and the Son of Man standing at the right hand of God!" (7:56).

That confession of confidence contained all that he had tried to say about Jesus and the one thing the leaders of Israel abhorred most.

To say that Jesus was the Messiah of the Jews was one thing; to claim that He was the Son of God was worse; but to give Him the title Son of Man was more than they could tolerate. To them that meant that Jesus was the Savior of the whole world. The term "Son of Man" encompassed the Ezekiel passages and signaled that God's Messiah would save all people, not just the Jews. Loss of exclusiveness and the depreciation of their own distinct identity as God's only people was what they feared most. If Jesus was Son of Man, that spelled the beginning of the end of their priority and special privilege. No wonder they cried out in uncontrollable hatred. The truth had cut too closely.

The Church's First Martyr

After Stephen was beaten by the enraged officers themselves, he was bound and dragged outside the city walls. (After all, the law commanded that no blood be spilled in the sacred precincts!) They pushed him over the wall and down into the pit in which he would be stoned. Saul stood by, keeping everything in good Deuteronomic order.

The witnesses against Stephen, according to the rule, were to be the first to throw the stones. These witnesses were carefully checked by Saul as they laid their outer garments at the Pharisee's feet (7:58). He watched as the first heavy stones struck Stephen's face. That face! It still had the same radiance, confidence, and love Saul had observed earlier. Then he heard Stephen's strong, courageous voice cry out, not for mercy or to compromise his beliefs in the hope of saving himself, but in prayer to his Lord. Who would pray at a time like this? Saul's heart was now a bit ambivalent. What was it about this Stephen? His name, *Stephanos*, in Greek meant "crown," and now his "crown" was the unmistakable radiance that hallowed his face.

As the stones rained down upon him, Stephen prayed, "Lord, do not hold this sin against them." Then he died. The crowd was silent. In that moment the potent compound of relief, guilt, fear of death itself, and the uneasiness of having taken judgment into their own hands filled the air. And Saul was there watching.

God Brings Good Out of Evil

In order to appreciate fully the meaning of Stephen's martyrdom, we need to live in the skins of both the members of the Church and of those who persecuted them.

The questions the followers of the Master must have asked are on our lips. *Lord, why did You let this happen?* If You were there with Stephen, with all the authority and power of the living God, why didn't You intercede and save him? Is prayer only for strength and never for deliverance? The questions echo through the ages and resound in our own hearts. Why do good people suffer? Why do potential leaders like Stephen get snuffed out as their flame blazes so brightly?

That's what the early Church must have asked as they huddled behind locked doors for fear they would be next, or in prison wondering why they were not spared in the name of Jesus. Stephen had been the hope of the future. He had been the leader of a new wave of leadership to follow after the apostles. Would there be hope for future generations, or would they all come to the same end? The early believers overestimated the power of their enemies and underestimated the power of the Lord, just as we sometimes do. God was not finished; He had barely begun.

Getting inside the feelings of the early Church must be combined with getting inside Saul. We can only wonder what went through Saul's mind as he stood watching. One thing is certain: Stephen's death showed him that he was not dealing with ordinary people. Later in Acts we see that the Lord of the movement Saul was trying to stamp out was closing in on him. On the way to Damascus to rout out and persecute the followers there, Saul was possessed by the memory of Stephen and the inextinguishable fire he had witnessed in the Master's men and women. That indelible impression began a civil war within the vigilant Pharisee. He was already prepared to respond when the Lord Himself intercepted him on the road and revealed Himself undeniably alive. What might have happened if Stephen had been a man who could be bought at the price of safety or survival?

But go deeper. The persecution of the Church in Jerusalem caused believers to scatter throughout Judea and Samaria and, later, to all the then-known world. Stephen's message had declared the independence of the Church from remaining a sect of Judaism; now his death forced an independence of the Church from Jerusalem. This was the beginning of Christianity's thrust into the Gentile world, where the Church would be forced to see that Christ was the Savior of the world. And the one who had executed Stephen would become the acknowledged new leader of missionary Christianity.

How the Lord moves! He's always there making good out of evil. God took the very one who sought to destroy the Church and made him the greatest declarer of the gospel. Little did Stephen know that his death would become a mighty wind that would blow the seed pod open and plant seeds not only in the heart of his chief opponent, but across the world to bear a millionfold harvest through the centuries. Stephen's character and resultant countenance were forever an example to Saul (henceforth called "Paul" in Acts) of what Christ can do in a person's life.

Years later, Augustine wrote an answer to the deepest questions in our hearts as to why the Lord allowed Stephen to suffer and die: "If St. Stephen had not spoken thus, if he had not prayed thus, the Church would not have had Paul." The blood of the martyrs is indeed the seed of the Church. Little did Saul know as he guarded the coats of the witnesses who stoned Stephen that he soon would wear the mantle of Stephen himself!

Learning from Stephen
The account of Stephen's martyrdom leaves us with some convicting conclusions. First, the Lord does not offer us safety, but He does offer us strength. Our task is obedience to Christ. This obedience may lead to difficulty, but He will give us power to stand in the midst of all that happens to us.

Second, if we have been purchased by the blood of the Cross, we have been purchased for keeps. The Lord's forgiving love convinces us that we belong to Him, and nothing is worth more than that. Yet we all know the bitter experience of being tempted to deny our faith or auction off our convictions for the sake of our reputations. Remember that the Lord never lets go of what He has purchased at the high cost of the Cross. He steps in repeatedly to reclaim His possessions and confirm that we are His.

Third, this passage tells us that our Lord is unrelentingly working out His purposes through the worst things that happen to us. He is not absent during difficulties. He will use them to bring us into deeper fellowship with Him. He will also use what we go through to reveal to others what He is able to do in the excruciating trials of their own lives.

It's hard not to wonder what we would have done in Stephen's place. We probably would have sold out—*unless* we had had the same gifts of the Holy Spirit Stephen had. And of course we do. From Stephen's example we are forced to ask ourselves:

- ◆ Have I allowed the indwelling Spirit to give me the gift of faith to trust Jesus completely and to dare unreservedly?
- ◆ Have I accepted the gift of grace in order to become a truly gracious person whom no manner of evil can defeat?
- ◆ Am I open to being a riverbed for the flow of the Spirit's power to enable me and others to experience the immeasurable vitality of God in each situation?
- ◆ Is there evidence in my life and speech that I have the gift of wisdom?
- ◆ Can I look deeply into the mysteries of God and have knowledge of Him and discernment of His guidance for myself and those around me?
- ◆ Are there signs and wonders trailing my footsteps—people loved, healed, introduced to the Savior?
- ◆ Am I the one who can step into the breach of human frustration and impotence and bring the hope of the Lord?
- ◆ What do people see in my countenance and face?

Did the Lord do for Stephen what He is unwilling to do for us? Hardly. The point is that Stephen did not start out with a strategy to redirect the course of history. Most great people God uses never do. On a human level, Stephen was not any greater than you or I. The difficulties he went through brought out what the Lord had worked into his character.

If we are willing to be as open to the Holy Spirit as Stephen was, then we will be trusted with the kinds of opportunities and challenges he was. But we won't see this as trouble; we will be able to allow life to happen to us fully. Instead of resisting reality, we can befriend it, knowing the Lord will use it. Make this your prayer: "Lord, give me Your Holy Spirit; pour into me faith, grace, power, wisdom, and freedom to believe You can do signs and wonders in and around me. Then give me whatever challenges You can use to bless others and expand Your Church."

7

The Adventurous Life

Following the Spirit's Guidance

Acts 8:26-40

I believe there is a secret to living an adventurous life. People who have discovered it are some of the most attractive, winsome people I know. Their lives are distinguished by eagerness and earnestness. They have zest and zeal.

The mysterious origin of this vitality is traceable to two words: *guidance* and *obedience*. The Bible teaches that the Holy Spirit actually can guide our thoughts and that our obedience can appropriate His power to do what is guided. The wonder of all this stems from the amazing fact that the Holy Spirit can put into our minds ideas, insights, possibilities, and directions that we would never have conceived or dared contemplate without Him.

R. H. L. Sheppard put it this way: "Christianity does not consist in abstaining from doing things no [one] would think of doing, but in doing things that are unlikely to occur to anyone who is not in touch with the Spirit of Christ." When I first read these words, it was as though a current of electricity surged through me. *That's it!* I thought. There's the secret: not just abstinence, but affirmation. A Christ-honed conscience can guide our morals, ethics, and personal behavior. That's maintenance. But what about adventure?

The real adventure begins when we love the Lord with our minds and dare to believe that He can invade our cerebral cortex to guide our thinking, imagination, and will. When we are filled with the Holy Spirit, there is an inspiring infusion of His thoughts into our thinking. He becomes the Lord of our intelligence and imagination, the generator of the mind's potency for possibilities we never dreamed could be. Couple that with the will to act on and follow the Holy Spirit's leading, and you have the secret of exciting living.

Philip Follows Orders

This same secret of supernatural leading is written across the pages of the book of Acts. That's what made Philip such a powerful witness. He was guided by the Holy Spirit, and he was obedient. In Acts 8 we discover why he was so effective. Our goal in considering this passage of Scripture is to uncover how the Spirit wants to work in and through us today.

Following Stephen's death, a wave of persecution against the Church in Jerusalem forced many to flee to Judea and Samaria. We then meet the deacon Philip as he "went down to the city of Samaria and proclaimed the Messiah to them" (Acts 8:5). The Samaritans were considered half-breeds and looked down upon by orthodox Jews. Yet Philip faithfully preached, and the Lord performed many miracles that resulted in the Samaritans receiving the gospel.

Let's look specifically at Luke's next account in Acts 8:26-40. This passage shows us that when the Spirit controls our minds, we are open, ready, and available. An angel of the Lord gave Philip very clear orders to "'Get up and go toward the south to the road that goes down from Jerusalem to Gaza.' (This is a wilderness road)" (vs. 26). Note that Philip did not ask why or what he was to do when he got there. Most of us would have wanted a detailed briefing with everything planned down to the last minutiae. Not Philip. He knew the exciting secret of obedience: "So he got up and went."

Dynamic Christian living is capsulized in these few words. The fact that he "got up" says to me that he had been sitting down; or, more consistent with Luke's intended message, I imagine he got up from his prayer knees and went to do what he was told. Philip was a God-called, filled, guided, and sent man of power.

Don't miss several crucial things about these verses. One, God does guide His people. He gets through to us by inspiring thoughts and directions. In this portion of Acts, Philip is instructed by an angel and later by the Spirit (vs. 29). An angel is a messenger of God; the Spirit is the immediacy of God at work in the mind and soul. The point is that Philip was a cooperative person who could both hear and respond to the influence and instruction of the living God. That same possibility exists for you and me.

Now observe a second insight. Philip was given just enough guidance to change his plans and go in a new direction. What trust and flexibility! The Lord guides us both into and in the situations He has prepared for us. It takes raw courage to obey in one without being sure of the other. Often we are given just enough guidance to take the first step. Philip obeyed because he believed that the Lord knew what He was doing and could leave the results to Him.

Timing Is Everything

Philip was not only given direction where to go but also when to go. His obedience was important because of the Lord's timing. "Get up and go toward the south," the angel directed. Philip did not need to be told that the road from Jerusalem to Gaza went south; that was common knowledge. The crucial issue was *when*. The Greek word which is translated "south" in our text usually means "midday or noon." ("Get up and go at noon" is offered as a footnote alternative in some versions.) The Lord wanted Philip on that road at a particular time for what He was preparing. I am utterly amazed that Philip did not say, "Midday, Lord? On that sun-blistered road in the desert? You'd better level with me. What are you up to?"

Perhaps the reason many of us miss out on the great things God has prepared is because we miss His timing. Think of the opportunities we have never experienced because we were immobilized on dead center waiting for the "big picture" before we would do the Lord's will. Philip didn't wait.

The startling fact is that Philip's willingness to be positioned on that road at that time and place made possible the miracle of the transformation of a human being. Guidance is relational. It grows out of a relationship with the Holy Spirit, and it usually results in the blessing of a relationship in which He wants us to be His person and to communicate His love and hope.

The Spirit's timing was perfect that day on the desert road to Gaza. The secretary of the treasury of the Candace Dynasty of Ethiopia was also on that road. Luke paints a vivid portrait of the man, giving us both his outward circumstances and his inner condition. We can picture this African leader riding in his stately chariot surrounded by the accoutrements of position and power. A eunuch, he had risen to great influence serving the Queen of Ethiopia. But all the outward manifestations of courtly pomp did not satisfy the longings of his inner being.

That hunger brought him under the influence of monotheistic Judaism. It seems certain that he had become a proselyte Jew. His longing for truth and reality had prompted him to make a journey to Jerusalem, the center of Hebrew religion and culture. We are told that he had "come to worship" (vs. 27). The Greek literally means that he was on a pilgrimage.

Everything Luke tells us about the Ethiopian indicates that the temple, the sacrifices, and the rehearsal of ancient customs had not fed the spiritual hunger in him. But the Lord knew his need. He had brought him to Jerusalem, not for what he could find there, but for what he would experience on the road home with a young man who had the clarity of the gospel in his head and the fire of the Holy Spirit in his heart. Philip and the treasurer of Ethiopia met on the road by the Spirit's design. The eunuch's disappointment with Jerusalem would be superseded by the Lord's appointment.

The Spirit's Guidance

The story moves quickly. Philip receives the next stage of guidance. He had been open to go; now he understood why. When he saw the chariot moving slowly ahead of him, the Spirit spoke to Philip—another example of God's remarkable power to break into thought and conceive an idea! The Spirit said, "Go over to this chariot and join it." The Greek words unlock the astounding admonition; they mean "join yourself to; be glued to." The impact is clear: Philip was to get next to this awesome-appearing leader, focus his total attention on him, and become united to his need. I wonder if Philip thought, *Lord, now I know why you sent me here at this moment!* We cannot be sure, but what we can discern is that in keeping with his Spirit-enabled responsiveness, Philip probably prayed as he was climbing into the chariot, "Lord, use me. Tell me what to say. Make me sensitive, open, contagious."

A prayer like that must have been offered because of the obvious way the Spirit guided Philip's words. The guidance of the Holy Spirit is never more effective or evident than when He uses us to communicate the love and forgiveness of God through Christ to another. Allow the Spirit to use what He did in Philip then to thunder a stirring thought in your heart now. He can guide what you say in the situations and relationships of your life.

Note the progression of the Spirit's guidance and of Philip's response. In each step we can discover what He wants to give us today.

1. Philip listened.

The Spirit's most sensitive guidance is often *not* to speak too quickly. Philip had patience. He did not climb into the chariot and begin a prewritten oration about salvation. Instead, as he listened, he overheard the Ethiopian reading from a scroll of the prophet Isaiah, which he had probably purchased in Jerusalem. He was reading the words over and over again. The same Spirit guiding Philip was guiding the eunuch to one of the most crucial passages of Hebrew Scripture, Isaiah 53, the clear prediction of the suffering Messiah:

> Like a sheep he was led to the slaughter,
> and like a lamb silent before its shearer,
> so he does not open his mouth.
> In his humiliation justice was denied him.
> Who can describe his generation?
> For his life is taken away from the earth.

2. Philip asked a question.

This was the second step of the Spirit's guidance. Instead of saying, "An Ethiopian like you probably doesn't understand what Isaiah is talking about. I've been sent here to straighten you out," Philip was led to question with authentic concern, "Do you understand what you are reading?" (vs. 29). He got into the Ethiopian's "space" and felt with him the longings of his heart. Note that Philip was neither put off by nor overly impressed with the man's stature or wealth. His question was drenched with love and tender helpfulness.

Only the Spirit can help us to come alongside another person and catch the impact of what that person is thinking or hoping. Gentle questions guided by the Holy Spirit communicate interest, esteem, affirmation, and encouragement to another person. I have witnessed hundreds of people come to the experience of Christ through love expressed by people who genuinely wanted to know about them and their needs. Friends, fellow workers, "chance" acquaintances at parties have felt the impact of grace through inquiring questions that helped them know that someone cared, was interested in them, and had something to share, but in the context of their particular concern.

3. Philip knew the Scriptures.

As a fulfilled Hebrew, Philip knew the hope of Isaiah 53 and the completion of that hope in Jesus, the Messiah. Philip moved right out onto the edge of discovery to which the Spirit had guided the Ethiopian. He neither changed the subject to something on his agenda, nor did he redirect the conversation to present Christ in his favorite fashion. The most effective way to present Christ is to pick up where people are in their search for reality through some religion, philosophy, cult, or contemporary spiritual fad.

Some time ago, a woman related to me the virtues of transcendental meditation. She told me about being given a mantra, or magic word, to repeat in her twice-daily, fifteen-minute meditation. A mantra is defined as a thought, the effects of which are known. The word, she said, led her into deep identification with herself and reality. I affirmed her search. Then the Spirit gave me a question that a thousand hours of planning and preparation for that conversation could never have prompted. "Does the word you are using put you in touch with the limitless power that created the universe?" Immediately she wanted to know *my* "word." More than a mantra—the name of Jesus Christ!

But she could never have heard me or subsequently given her life to the Savior and learned to pray in His name if I had not affirmed her and her urgent search for peace. The Spirit can and does guide our conversations. And yet that evening when I was getting ready to go to the party where I met this woman, I had no idea what the Spirit had been preparing. I had felt impelled to go in spite of my desire to have an evening at home. Someone once said, "Stop praying and the coincidences stop happening."

The fact that Philip knew the Isaiah Scriptures indicates that God had been preparing the way long before he received guidance to go south. I am convinced that Philip's instruction in the Scriptures before he accepted Christ and his later instruction in the Church under the scripturally astute apostles was all for this moment with the eunuch.

What an exciting thing it is to realize that the Spirit is not bound by time or space! He can use the preparation of the past for present effectiveness and is ubiquitously on the move to utilize what has happened for what He wants to happen. That's the mystery of the guided life.

The Ethiopian's response to Philip's question indicated that his previous pleas for help had gone unheeded. He responded to the question with a pitiful plea of his own, "How can I, unless someone guides me?" Philip utilized the moment. He helped the Nubian pilgrim understand that the One about whom Isaiah spoke was the Savior of the world and could be his Savior. Philip told him the good news of what God had done in Christ and what that meant in his own experience.

4. Philip did not pressure.

The Spirit's guidance liberated Philip from pushing the man too hard. He did not feel compelled to "close the deal" with urgent sales techniques. He trusted the Spirit's work in the eunuch. When they came to a pool of water, surely Philip saw the water beside the road before the potential convert did. But he waited, and, I'm sure, he prayed.

Listen to the Spirit-prompted longing in the Ethiopian, "Look, here is water! What is to prevent me from being baptized?" This was surely the Holy Spirit's movement. How much more lasting is a conversion that has been motivated from within by the Spirit rather than manipulated from without by ritual compulsion.

The eunuch was baptized and entered eternal life, for which Jesus, the Lamb of God about whom he had been reading, had died and was raised up to give him. God had the pilgrim from Ethiopia in mind all along: in a crèche in Bethlehem, a Cross on Calvary, a Spirit-empowered Church in Jerusalem, a vulnerable, readable deacon, a road to Gaza, Scriptures written hundreds of years before, the water beside the road, and a baptism into life. The Lord who made and redeemed the universe is alive, doing all things well through the Holy Spirit.

But not without you and me as irreplaceable channels of His love and power. The Lord of all creation has ordained that He will do His work through us. As we seek His guidance and obey what He wants us to do and say, He works through us to bless the world.

This chain of blessing necessitates becoming acquainted with the Spirit and discovering how to listen and respond. Nothing is more crucial than that—for ourselves, for people around us, for the church, for a society aching for solutions to problems only the Spirit can unravel. In his book *The Cost of Discipleship*, Dietrich Bonhoeffer states, "Only he who believes obeys and only he who obeys believes." We cannot grow in belief unless we obey what we have been guided to do as a result of what we believe already. Guidance and obedience must be kept together.

Ask to Be Filled

To nail down what this passage says to us today, we need to identify the building blocks of an adventurous life following the Spirit's lead. The first building block is to be filled with the Spirit. Philip was a man "full of the Holy Spirit" (Acts 6:3) and therefore he could be guided by the Spirit. Preparation for the Gaza road incident began when, long before, the Spirit took possession of his mind and heart.

Our capacity to be guided is in direct proportion to our faithful receptivity to the Holy Spirit. If we have allowed Him to guide our thoughts in the past, He will help us specifically in the present. It's easier to steer a moving vehicle than one that is stopped. If we are on the move in the Spirit, He can guide us more easily. So the first step to becoming a guided person is to ask to be filled with the Holy Spirit.

Many present-day Christians miss out here. We go to God for guidance about problems as if we could plug in and out of the flow of wisdom. We wring our hands asking, "Lord, what do you want me to do?" Often when we seek guidance, it's a sure sign that we are out of it! The Lord wants to get us to the place where we are constantly in touch with Him, allowing our minds to receive and act on His thoughts and direction. Then He can guide us naturally, momentarily, persistently. Getting guidance then is not a crisis. He has been working in us before the crisis occurs. If we are constantly besieging Him with some new emergency that has occurred because we have been out of fellowship with Him, we probably will not be open to the surprises He wants to work through us.

Set Your Mind on the Spirit

The second building block I see in this passage is to trust the Spirit's leading. Philip trusted the Spirit and did not try to distinguish between his own desires and the Spirit's direction. There was a glorious indistinction between his thoughts and the instructions of the Spirit. He dared to believe that the Spirit within him could be trusted.

So often the self-condemning mistrust we have of our insights and ideas blocks out the guidance the Spirit is trying to give. But if we have surrendered our minds to Him, we can dare to honor our thoughts. The apostle Paul knew this secret. He distinguished between the mind set on the Spirit and the mind set on the flesh. The *flesh* is a biblical word for humanity separated from the love and power of God. A mind set on the flesh is one dependent on human training, learning, experience, and insight. In that light, consider the distinction Paul makes in Romans 8:5-8:

For those who live according to the flesh set their minds on the things of the flesh, but those who live according to the Spirit set their minds on the things of the Spirit. To set the mind on the flesh is death, but to set the mind on the Spirit is life and peace. For this reason the mind that is set on the flesh is hostile to God; it does not submit to God's law—indeed it cannot, and those who are in the flesh cannot please God.

The person in Christ is liberated from that. His or her mind belongs to Christ and is indwelt by His Spirit. Now reflect on Paul's description of a person who has received the mind of Christ:

But you are not in the flesh; you are in the Spirit, since the Spirit of God dwells in you. Anyone who does not have the Spirit of Christ does not belong to him. But if Christ is in you, though the body is dead because of sin, the Spirit is life because of righteousness. If the Spirit of him who raised Jesus from the dead dwells in you, he who raised Christ from the dead will give life to your mortal bodies also through his Spirit that dwells in you. (Rom. 8:9-11)

Living in the Spirit does away with the feverish frenzy to decide what is *our* selfish thought and what is the Spirit's guidance. Bottom line summation gives us the total truth: "For all who are led by the Spirit of God are children of God" (Rom. 8:14). That means you and me, praise God!

The Lord has given us reliable checkpoints for evaluating the authenticity of what we feel prompted to do or say. Here are some questions I ask myself:

- Is it consistent with Christ? Does it contradict His message in any way?
- Will it express love and bring the ultimate good of all concerned? (Note, I say *ultimate* because often we are guided to do hard things that bring temporary pain or conflict but are part of our own or another person's growth.)
- Will it bring me into deeper fellowship with Christ? Can I do it with Him there beside me?

- ◆ Are my motives pure? Is it manipulative?
- ◆ Will it extend the kingdom? Will I be able to look back on it, free of guilt, self-incrimination, or regret?

Added to these questions is the assurance that if we fail or misfire, there is forgiveness and a chance to begin again. So why not trust the Spirit to guide us?

Listen to the Spirit's Prompting

That leads us to the third building block. Being led by the Spirit requires a sensitive "ear" in our minds. We need to say constantly what Samuel prayed: "Speak, Lord, for your servant hears." That prayer is the motto of an exciting, Spirit-guided life. It is the secret of the adventure.

The Spirit prompts us to think about something or someone. Most of us find that our greatest concerns involve people. We want God's maximum best for them. That's where a very special gift is given to a Spirit-filled person. The gift of prophecy enables us to know what God is doing in people and their circumstances. It is a penetrating X-ray vision to see beneath the surface. But it is always coupled with clarity about what to do and say. God is not a God of confusion but of peace (1 Cor. 14:33) in the imparting of this precious gift. The prompting of the Spirit's guidance comes in practical ways. Say this; write that letter; make that phone call; send that gift; make that visit; do that act out of love with no thought of reward. To refuse is fatal.

Respond in Obedience

The fourth and final thing I've learned from Philip follows naturally: God's results are dependent upon our response. What would have happened if Philip had said he would rather stay in Jerusalem with the fellowship of the apostles? The early church historian Eusebius claims that the Ethiopian, whom he calls by the name of Indich, became a Christian leader, brought the good news of the gospel to Ethiopia, and was the founder of a strong church that grew there. Not just Indich, but Ethiopia was at stake in Philip's response.

We have seen the results of what cooperating with the Spirit can mean for us and others. But we also know what happens when we refuse. We are painfully aware of the existential truth that God will not bypass His chosen human agents. He has willed it so. If we resist, havoc—or what's worse, dull mediocrity—results.

I think of a father and daughter who were deadlocked in hostile silence after a family conflict. Both were wrong. The man prayed that the Lord would straighten out his daughter. One day he felt the Lord say, "Go to your daughter and apologize for your judgmentalism." The father refused and the drawn swords continued. Then one day this man came across Paul's words in the Bible, "Fathers, do not provoke your children to anger, but bring them up in the discipline and instruction of the Lord" (Eph. 6:4). The Spirit impressed on him, "If you do not do what I have told you to do, you will not grow in the Christian life." Finally he obeyed, and healing resulted. His confession brought openness and confession from his daughter, and the two were reconciled.

A woman I know became nearly hysterical about what was happening to her daughter and her grandchildren because her son-in-law was not a Christian believer. She would nag and press him with her urgent desire for his conversion. One day, thinking about the situation, a new thought came to her mind: "Be to your son-in-law what you hope he will become. Leave his conversion to the Lord. Stop sending tracts and literature. Think of five things you like about him, emphasize them and affirm him." From the time she dared to accept that guidance, life-transforming character changes began to emerge in the young husband.

Recently a friend of mine had my wife on her mind. She couldn't let it drop. "Lord, what do you want me to do?" she prayed. That day she had a "chance" conversation with a medical doctor whose specialty was the type of cancer my wife was battling with at that time. He asked if it would help if he called us to give encouragement, which he did. He was a great help and gave us timely advice on the very day we desperately needed it. God had arranged the whole thing because He loves us!

Another man was in a chronically sick marriage. He and I prayed about it constantly. But he had received more light than he was willing to walk in. He had prayed that the Lord would solve the sexual difficulties in his marriage. For him the intimacy of sex was a vital expression of sexual desire; for his wife it was an expression of response to tenderness and warmth in the total ambience of their life together. Through some creative reading and counseling, the Spirit went to work teaching him that gratification was not his right; that giving sensitive, tender affirmation was his responsibility. Finally one day he yielded his mind to the Spirit's leading. Each time he was given an urge from the Spirit to do and say the gracious, loving thing, he obeyed. His wife said, "Instead of a penthouse panther, I've got a lover! I don't know what happened, but I like it. My husband has changed."

These stories of real people dramatize the secret of an exciting life—following the Spirit's lead. He knows not only the past and present, but the future; not only what we need, but what we will need; not only our own concerns, but those of others. And He has chosen us to do His work in the world. The Holy God, Creator of all, Savior and Lord, will use you and me. We can cooperate with Him in accomplishing His plans and purposes in people and situations. Now that's living!

8
When the Answer Keeps Knocking

Acts 12

Prayer begins with God through the instigation and inspiration of the Holy Spirit. The Holy Spirit seeks to give us a special gift for courageous praying: expectation. With the gift of expectation we can pray with boldness and hope; without it our prayers become perfunctory. Sometimes we get to the place where we pray but do not expect an answer. That's especially true in our intercessory prayers for people.

When most of us think about praying for other people's needs, our minds leap to something we want God to do or change. We immediately see the yawning gap between who they are and who they should be, what they have and what they need, what they have done and what they ought to do. We envision prayer as the bridge between what is and what ought to be. We have learned that God's abundant resources are available for people if we will pray, and that is good. But I want to focus on the power of prayer for *appreciation* as well as anticipation.

There is a profound level of prayer that goes beyond remission for what is past or requests for what we long to be for the people we love. In-depth prayer for people liberates us to enjoy them right now, where they are, as they are. William Law was right: "There is nothing which makes us love a man so much as praying for him." And prayer-born love frees us to recognize that the person is himself or herself God's greatest answer to prayer.

The early Church had a difficult time comprehending this truth in their prayers for Peter. They could not apprehend what God had appropriated. The beloved leader of the Church was imprisoned by King Herod Agrippa I, probably in the Temple of Antonia. The king knew that persecution of Christians would strengthen his relationship with the Jews. His execution of the apostle James had won him the favor of the turbulent people whose approval he desperately needed. Peter was next. But while Agrippa pondered the most expeditious method for executing Peter, the Church prayed. Nothing had been too great for their Lord! But did they still believe that? This passage of Acts makes us wonder.

Somebody's Knocking at the Door

Luke impresses us with the humanly impossible situation through the context of the prayers of the Church to the Lord for Peter. In Acts 12 we are told that Herod seized him and put him in prison with no fewer than four squads to guard him. That means sixteen soldiers divided into four watches, each of three hours' duration. "The very night when Herod was going to bring him out [for execution, the Greek implies], Peter, bound with two chains, was sleeping between two soldiers, while guards in front of the door were keeping watch over the prison" (Acts 12:6). Picture a soldier on each side of the sleeping saint, probably as many as four sentries at the door of the cell, and soldiers from the squads strategically positioned—an imposing sight of human power and precaution. Herod was taking no chances.

Neither was the Church! They prayed that a greater power would intercede to help Peter. But Luke does not tell us how or for what they prayed. Did they pray that Peter would be strong even to death? Perhaps they prayed that he would be able to witness to the guards. Some may have prayed for a miraculous release. But did they really believe it could happen? That question is forced upon us by the amazing fact that when God answered their prayers, they did not, at first, believe what had happened.

In response to the Church's intercession, the Lord interceded. He sent an angel who liberated Peter from his chains, led him past the first and second guards, and opened the iron gate of the prison leading out to the city. As the incarnate answer to prayers, Peter headed directly for John Mark's house, where the Lord's people had gathered in the memory-filled Upper Room to pray. A stone wall separated the house and gardens from the street. A heavy wooden gate provided the only way inside. Peter paused at the gate and knocked. A maid named Rhoda was delegated by the intercessory fellowship to see who had come to interrupt their prayers. She recognized Peter's voice when he implored her to open the gate, but she was so befuddled by the personified answer to their prayers that she could not open the gate. She ran back to the Upper Room to tell the praying disciples that Peter was at their gate!

Now grapple with their unbelieving response. They said to her, "You are out of your mind!" (vs. 15). When she persisted, they expressed incredulity another way: "It is his angel." This response implies human nature's capacity to expect the worst. The disciples actually entertained the dreadful possibility that Peter had been executed and his ghost had come to them. Or perhaps, in keeping with the idea held at this time that each person had a guardian angel, they concluded that Peter's angel was there to comfort them about the excruciating eventuality. Whatever the case, they did not believe it was Peter. The Church was so engrossed in praying for Peter that they could not accept Peter!

"Meanwhile Peter continued knocking" (vs. 16). The answer to the Church's prayers kept waiting for a response. We have to be amazed when we contemplate the insensitivity of the Church. But then the truth hits us where we hurt. Who is our Peter for whom we have prayed, and what lack of faith keeps him or her waiting and knocking at the gate? Many of us would rather go on praying than accept God's answer. What if Peter had not kept on knocking? It was dangerous for him to stand out in the street; he could have been arrested again.

What would the Church have done then? Would they have dared to go back to prayer for a second miracle when they had not accepted the first? Surely they would, for we do it all the time. Perhaps that's why our prayers are so empty and habitually unexpectant.

God Can Do Anything

This passage of Acts tells us a lot about the prayer life of the early Church and more than we may want to know about our own. In my own life, the Lord has used this passage to expose not only what I have done with the gift of prayer, but also what I do with the gifts that come from praying.

The first thing I learned is that my prayers are often limited to my preconceptions of what I think God will do. I am forced to wonder what it would take to convince me that with God all things are possible. I am sometimes like the early Church. So much had happened to those followers of Jesus in that Upper Room. There in John Mark's home they had received the Last Supper, had realized the presence of the resurrected Lord, and had been rejuvenated by the power of Pentecost. Miraculous answers to prayer attended the early years of the Church's growth. As we noted in a previous chapter, they had prayed for boldness and the room had been shaken with power.

But the years had wilted their expectancy. The account of their reaction to Peter's reappearance clearly indicates that they either had not dared to pray for his release; or if they had, they anticipated that it might not happen. Why else would they be surprised and incredulous? But are we any different? I'm not, too much of the time. Do you share the problem? Are your prayers limited to the careful confines of what you think God can do?

The core cause of the Church's unadventuresome prayers, perhaps, is that they believed more about the formidable power of people than they believed about the unlimited power of God. The prison and the guards—who could escape that? And look at James; he didn't escape. The pall of his execution hung heavily on the Church. The same thing would probably happen to Peter. Why pray for release? They lost the two-dimensional formula for great praying: daring requests and unreserved relinquishment. They had the latter, but forgot the first. They trusted Peter to God and prayed for him, but did not ask for his miraculous release. The comforting thing about that, however, is that even their halting, doubting prayers were mightier than Herod.

Many of us are afraid of bold prayers because we do not want to be embarrassed by an answer that is less than or different from what we asked. We feel we must protect God's reputation by never getting out on a limb with requests which may not be granted. Our faith is so frail that we feel we cannot afford a disappointment, which would snap the thin thread of our hope that He is real, that He hears and answers prayer.

The combination of unreserved petition and unrestrained trust in the Lord's timing and wisdom makes for dynamic praying. He alone knows what's best for us, the Church, and our times. His answers are "Yes," "No," or "Later"; but a loving providence guides all three! All we need to do is think of some of the things for which we prayed that we now see would not have been good for us if they had been granted. With that confidence we can pray with freedom and joy, knowing that the Lord will answer according to His overarching benevolence.

Are You Ready for the Answer?

A second thing I discovered in this passage is that sometimes we are so occupied in praying for an answer that we can't recognize it when it comes. That was the problem with the early Church's prayers for Peter. The Lord interrupted their prayer time for Peter with the apostle himself. They weren't ready for that! We seem to find comfortable security in persistent, preoccupied praying about a problem. The familiar feeling of distress over a difficulty or a need becomes more satisfying than the answer.

This fact is especially true when the answer demands that *we* become part of God's answer to a prayer. Often the prayers complain more about people than they confess our trust in God. We complain to God about what needs to be changed or corrected in someone. But then we find it demands too much when we are asked to affirm the changes that occur.

That's what happened to a group of people who were concerned about their pastor. They decided to pray, "Lord, revive him or re-move him!" Quite sure that it would be the latter, they could not encourage the first alternative when it began to take place. They found greater pleasure in the problem than assurance in the answer.

A father I know prayed ceaselessly about his son. The young man's emotional problems were of grave concern to him. Then one day, he shared the problem with a friend. The response was not what he expected. "Unless you are willing to spend time with your son, all your praying will miss the mark! You are the answer to your own prayers. He needs you." But the father did not recognize the answer and kept on praying for his son to change. There are times we cannot gain a full vision from our prayers because we have not accepted the part of the answer that is staring us in the face. The complete un-folding of an answer to prayers awaits recognition of the portion of the answer that has been given.

A woman told me about a friend who was having difficulty han-dling life's relationships, and we prayed together about her friend. Later I asked how the friend was doing, and I heard real evidence of a change. But the woman had not seen her friend's first efforts to change as the beginning of God's answer. I asked her if she had af-firmed this initial attempt to reach out, and she admitted that she hadn't. She said that she had completely missed the importance of this change in her friend.

Think how often this is repeated in family life. Parents pray for their children but then let negativism completely dominate their attitude about changes in them. No wonder children become discour-aged in their efforts to respond to the nudgings of the Spirit and thus become the person their parents are praying they will become. This paradox is no less true of children's prayers for their parents or broth-ers and sisters. Andrew Murray said, "To be thankful for what I have received and for what my Lord has prepared is the surest way to receive more." Perhaps our unresponsiveness to the answers accounts for why so little happens as a result of our prayers for people.

Finding Joy in What God Does
Lastly, this passage has taught me something else even more crucial.

The Church was so intent in prayer for Peter that they did not *enjoy* Peter as the answer to their prayers. I can feel what Peter must have felt as he made his way through the dark streets of Jerusalem from prison to John Mark's house. Excitement must have grown within him as he realized that his release was the Lord's answer to the prayers of the Church. What joy and delight must have surged through him as he hurried through the night!

Perhaps he pictured what it would be like to burst into the Upper Room and have the fellowship break into an enthusiastic welcome and then prayers of praise. Perhaps he was even being a bit playful as he knocked on the gate, waiting to savor every moment of the realization of the Lord's answer. What great disappointment he must have felt when the Church found it so difficult to accept his living appearance as the answer to their prayers. After first arguing with Rhoda, when they finally did open the gate, they found it difficult to enter into the triumph of Peter's homecoming.

Luke often tells us a great deal by what he leaves out. In every other evidence of the Lord's gracious intercession he records the Church's doxology of praise and adoration. There is no mention this time of delight and exultation in the Church's response to Peter's liberation. Most of all, there is no expression of enjoyment of Peter himself. The Church had not discovered that the purpose of prayer for a person is to break us open to relish the wonder of that person for who she or he is.

That presses me to ask, "How many of the people I pray for know how much I enjoy them? Has prayer for people released me to accept the awesome gift of each personality?" I am still learning what this means. Increasingly, prayers for people have become times of penetrating insight into the uniqueness and value of those people. When I understand that conversation with God about people is not only telling God about them but also allowing God to tell me what I need to know about those people, my prayers come alive. As I listen intently with an open mind and heart, I feel their struggle for identity, meaning, and fulfillment. I hear their hopes pulsating through their hurts. I see the real person trying to break free to love and care.

Let Christ Pray for You

I have discovered a way to pray for people that has paid off in sub-sequent encounters with them. In prayer, I try to use all my faculties to observe and hear the Lord pray for the person about whom I am praying. I picture our Lord praying with that person as the center of His concern. Then I listen to His loving intercession. My response is usually amazement. I learn things I never knew and gain insight that years of observation could never reveal.

This idea came to me from something Robert Murry McCheyne once said about prayer: "If I could hear Christ praying for me in the next room, I would not fear a million enemies. Yet distance makes no difference. He is praying for me." So I tried that and it filled me with new courage and hope about my own personal needs. Then I thought, *Why not try the same thing for other people? Why not "listen" to Jesus praying for them?* Then Romans 8:26 came to mind, "We do not know how to pray as we ought, but [the] very Spirit intercedes with sighs too deep for words." Our Lord not only prays for our needs, but also teaches us how to pray for others! The exciting thing is that then we can pray with new confidence because we know how to pray for the very things we have heard and felt the Lord praying for. There's the mysterious secret: First pray to know how to pray, and then pray for the things the Lord is more ready to give than we are to ask. I have never done that without receiving a fresh burst of delight and affirmation for the person about whom I have heard him pray.

To intercede means "to pass between." Christ is our eternal inter-cessor. From whom could we better learn to intercede according to the will of God? I have constantly rediscovered new warmth and graciousness for people as I have passed between them and the re-sourceful, limitless Lord. The result is profound gratitude not only for the Lord, but for the person I am bringing before Him.

Robert Louis Stevenson said, "I will think more of your prayers when I see more of your praises." Praise and prayer go together. If prayers for people do not lead to new praise to God for them and what He is doing in them, our prayers will become an evasion. The whole issue is: Do people feel our praise to God for them? Paul constantly thanked God for the people to whom he wrote his epistles. "I thank my God through Jesus Christ for all of you" (Rom. 1:8). "I give thanks to God always for you . . ." (1 Cor. 1:4). "I do not cease to give thanks for you, remembering you in my prayers . . ." (Eph. 1:16). "I thank my God in all my remembrance of you, always in every prayer of mine for you all making my prayer with joy, thankful for your partnership in the gospel from the first day until now" (Phil. 1:3-5). The same praise to God for people communicates esteem and appreciation in Paul's letters to the Thessalonians, to Timothy, and to Philemon. Has anyone ever read that in a letter from us or heard us say it to them?

All this centers on a powerful, convicting truth: *People themselves are God's answer to our prayers about them.* If that ever were communicated to them as a result of our prayers, a lot of the things we agonize about in prayer for them would be on the way to healing.

The answer keeps knocking. Peter's at the gate of the wall around our hearts that we've built up over the years for protection, privacy, individuality, separateness. But there is an opening and a gate. And people are knocking. Prayer sensitizes our ears to hear the knocking. Overtures of affection, pleas for help, cries of loneliness, eloquent silences that shout for attention, tender touches lest we forget the person exists, or angry outbursts leaping like flames from the cauldron of frustration within—all are knocks at the gate.

"Peter continued knocking"—I can't leave that until I have put in the place of Peter's name all the names and faces of the people knocking at my gate. Who are they for you? "And when they opened the gate, then they saw him and were amazed" (vs. 16). It's always that way: when we open the gateway of our hearts, we see the person for whom we have prayed. To see is to behold, to admire, to honor.

Elizabeth Barrett Browning in *Aurora Leigh* said, "God answers sharp and sudden on some prayers,/And thrusts the thing we have prayed for in our face." That's what happens when our prayers for some change or adjustment in a person's life are answered, not only in the particular thing for which we prayed, but when, in response to the Lord's love, we are thrust face to face and heart to heart with the person. And that's what we all want most of all, isn't it? In answer to our problem-oriented prayers, the Lord gives a person-centered answer. The answer keeps knocking until we accept the person as God's gracious gift.

9
Real Freedom, True Joy

Acts 13

How do you become a free person? I hear that question from people everywhere. Living in a free nation does not ensure personal freedom, nor does attending church. Being religious never made anyone free. We all know too many church members who are uptight, unloving, and chained to compulsive patterns and personality quirks. Sometimes we could be counted among them.

The bottom line of the gospel is freedom. God made the ultimate investment by sending His Son, Jesus Christ, into the world to live for us, die for our sins, and be raised up to live with us forever. The final measure of our experience of our Lord's love and forgiveness is whether or not it has liberated us from fear, guilt, the past, and self-negation, so that we can love Him, ourselves, and others.

Many of us are not free. We are incarcerated in prisons of our own making and the making of others. We are haunted by past hurts; we feel we must become good enough to deserve acceptance from God and others; we are afraid to express our true selves; we long for approval and affirmation; we constantly adjust our lives to ensure their flow; we ache for love and yet habitually do the things that make us seem unlovable.

Four people come into focus in my mind's eye. All have a spiritual freedom deficit in their lives. Though each of them is a Christian, when it comes to being life-affirming, loving, and lovable, the value of the gospel is almost washed out or counterbalanced by self-negation, debilitating memories, and inadequacy.

One person is a high school senior who does not like herself. Her family and friends have not helped reshape her self-image. She hangs on to past hurts from attempts to reach out to her peers that met with rejection. Now she is immobilized by fear. What would it mean for her to become free in Christ?

Another is a young man just out of graduate school. His relationship with his father has been demeaning, and his faith in Christ has not been enough to free him from the anger and hostility that he feels inside about what his father did to him. What would Christian freedom mean for him?

The third example is a compulsive people-pleaser. From childhood she learned that love must be earned. She feels she must constantly do something for her husband, children, and friends so that she will be worthy of their approval. She can never relax; her life is a constant stream of effort to assure a positive reaction from people. What would this person be like if she were set free by our Lord?

The final person is a master manipulator. His own insecure relationship with Christ forces him to work people like puppets. His job gives him great power, which he uses with equivocation and dissimulation to get people to perform. At home he is not very different. His wife and kids are rewarded when they do what he wants, when he wants it. When his patriarchal authority does not work, privileges are dangled like bait or material retaliation is threatened. How could a deeper experience of Christ free this manipulator to dare to motivate by love?

It is with these people in mind, and hosts of others like them, that I want to talk about what it means to be a free person. Perhaps you are like one of them or know someone who is. Maybe in your own way, you desire to discover a new or greater freedom. The purpose of this chapter is to meet these very pressing, practical needs for our emancipation through Christ.

A Formula for Freedom

Saul, the passionate Pharisee, provides a clear answer to the question of how to become a free person. The man who had been "breathing threats and murder against the disciples of the Lord," experienced a life-changing encounter with Jesus Christ, recounted for us in Acts 9. From that time on he was called Paul, and freedom in Christ became his banner call.

One of Paul's magnificent sermons is recorded in Acts 13:17-47. His words lead up to a triumphant conclusion in verses 38 and 39: "Let it be known to you therefore, my brothers, that through this man [Christ] forgiveness of sins is proclaimed to you; by this Jesus everyone who believes is set free from all those sins from which you could not be freed by the law of Moses."

There's a clear formula for this freedom. It declares what God has done, what we can receive, and what happens as a result. Catch the dynamic progression: the *faithfulness* of God, the *forgiveness* offered in Jesus Christ, the *faith* that grasps the gift, and the *freedom* that follows.

Paul came a long distance to proclaim the faithfulness of God in the Antioch synagogue. What happened to him along the way gave a ring of reality to his message. Months before, he and Barnabas along with Mark had left another Antioch in Syria and sailed to Cyprus on their first missionary journey. From Cyprus they sailed to Attalia, a seaport in the district of Pamphylia on the northern coast of the Mediterranean. Then they made their way a few miles to Perga. Here, two painful things happened to Paul that made his trust in the faithfulness of God into a fresh experience: John Mark defected the mission and the apostle contracted a physical disease. (Most scholars suggest that it must have been the malaria so prevalent in the lowlands around Perga; others suggest eye trouble.)

Paul was a sick man with a "thorn in his flesh" (2 Cor. 12:7) when he reached Antioch, but he would not turn back. This bold adventurer in Christ pressed on to preach the good news of the gospel.

Knowing the circumstances under which Paul preached his message about the faithfulness of God in the synagogue at Antioch gives us perspective on the kind of Christian freedom he proclaimed. It had an "in spite of" quality that precludes our ever saying, "That's fine for you, Paul, but you never knew the debilitating difficulties that keep *me* from that freedom!"

Christ Has Set Us Free

Paul became one of the freest men who ever lived. We find the root of his remarkable freedom in his convictions about Christ. Retracing history, Paul shows his listeners in the synagogue what God did through Christ to set His people free. He reminds them that the same Yahweh who called His people out of Egypt, gave them the Promised Land, and blessed the kingdom of Israel under David, was the Lord God who had come in the long expected Messiah, Jesus. With careful, scholarly detail he recounts the truth both of what God offered in the Messiah and how His people rejected the gift. His message rises in a crescendo as he reminds the people of the Crucifixion and the victory of the Resurrection. Paul declares that Christ was the full fruition of the faithfulness of God. There is no lasting freedom apart from Christ. Paul later wrote the Galatians, "For freedom Christ has set us free!" Christ alone was emancipation for him.

How do you become a free person? You must begin with a relationship with Christ or your freedom will have no real lasting power. All the things that keep us from being free people can be liberated by Him. Christ made that clear in His message, "If you continue in my word, you are truly my disciples, and you will know the truth and the truth will make you free" (John 8:31-32). The incredulous priests and Pharisees responded, "We are descendants of Abraham and have never been slaves to anyone. What do you mean by saying, 'You will be made free'?" Then Jesus gave the key to freedom: "Very truly, I tell you, everyone who commits sin is a slave to sin. . . . So if the Son makes you free, you will be free indeed" (John 8:34-36). The Son of God alone can set a person free from sin and guilt. The truth about Him and an experience of His love is the basis of true freedom. But how can this happen?

Forgiveness and Freedom Go Hand in Hand

Paul presses on to make the process clear. "Through this man for-giveness of sins is proclaimed to you" (vs. 38). Forgiveness and free-dom are inseparably linked. The faithfulness of God provided the Cross and Resurrection as the foundation of our freedom. Only a forgiven person is free.

We all know that truth from experience. The memory of past failures is like sand in the gears of our effectiveness. We are in the present what we have been in the past. The careful computer of memory records all the things we have done or have had done to us. We cannot wipe them out with redoubled efforts at goodness or self-justification. All that we have done to ourselves and others haunts us—until we are forgiven.

But the forgiveness must be radical and deep by One who has authority to forgive. Only an incarnate God upon the Cross can do that. "Forgive them; for they do not know what they are doing" (Luke 23:34). But we knew, Lord! And the voice of love that paid the price for our sins responds, "Neither do I condemn you. Go and sin no more" (John 8:11, NKJV). Can it be true? All that we have said and done, forgiven? Yes, even before we ask. It is love's priority and power to forgive. The psalmist found this:

> For you, O Lord, are good,
>   And ready to forgive,
> and abundant in mercy to all those
> who call upon you.
> (Ps. 86:5, NKJV)

The syndrome of failure, forgiveness, and repeated failure was finally broken in my life when I realized that I was forgiven even before I sinned and that there was nothing that I could do to make God stop loving me. My often reluctant request for forgiveness was grasping for a reality that had been finished for me on Calvary. The Cross did not change God's attitude toward me; it *revealed* His unchanging nature. That finally melted my compulsive, repetitive pattern and gave me my first true experience of freedom.

But there was no deep personal freedom until I forgave myself. The reason I kept on doing the things that caused me guilt was because I could not be as gracious to myself as God had been. Arrogant pride! I was playing God over my own life. I was shocked when a friend helped me see this. The bars of my own "guilt-ed cage" kept me locked in and unfree. Then one night in prayer I felt the Lord very near and powerful. "Will you love Lloyd as much as I do?" He asked. "Forgive him! I have."

Next to memories of our own failures, the thing that keeps most of us from becoming free people is our unwillingness to forgive others. The surest sign that we have received the forgiveness of God is our willingness to forgive people, past and present. C. S. Lewis was right: "Everyone says forgiveness is a lovely thing, until they have something to forgive."

The Lord's Prayer mocks our reluctance to forgive: "And forgive our sins—for we have forgiven those who sinned against us" (Luke 11:4, TLB). There is an undeniable equation here: we cannot fully experience the true forgiveness of God if we will not forgive. And our retort is, "I'll forgive, but I can't forget!" That's just another way of saying, "I can't forgive" when we keep going back over what someone said or did. Pride again. Stack that up against a God who says, "I will remember their sin no more" (Jer. 31:34). Our freedom is dependent on God's gift of a poor memory when it comes to others' failures.

Most of us need deep, remedial surgery on our memories of other people's sins, especially where they have frustrated or hurt us. Often it takes a loving friend to help us relive the pain, express our feelings, and give forgiveness. But only the divine power of the indwelling Holy Spirit can give us the motivation for true forgiveness. He alone can enable us to "be kind to one another, tenderhearted, forgiving one another, as God in Christ has forgiven you" (Eph. 4:32).

Faith Is the Foundation

Paul discloses the secret of that power to forgive: "By this Jesus everyone who believes is set free from all those sins from which you could not be freed by the law of Moses" (Acts 13:39). In this monumental statement in the synagogue at Antioch, the apostle used two of his favorite words: *pisteuō* ("believe")—closely related to *pistis* ("faith")—and *dikaioō* ("to set right with God on the basis of faith").

Freedom is not only the fruit of forgiveness, it is rooted in faith. This truth is the core of Paul's theology and the basis of the psychology of Christian freedom. Here is the "justification by faith alone" that Paul spells out repeatedly in his epistles. It is the good news of freedom for self-righteous, religious people. Faith alone, Paul asserts, can make a person acceptable before God. Our efforts will not make us good enough.

> For in it the righteousness of God is revealed through faith for faith; as it is written, 'The one who is righteous will live by faith.'. . . But now, apart from law, the righteousness of God has been manifested through faith in Jesus Christ for all who believe. For there is no distinction; since all have sinned and fall short of the glory of God, they are now justified by his grace as a gift, through the redemption which is in Christ Jesus. (Rom. 1:17; 3:21-24).

Martin Luther put it clearly: "Faith is a living, daring confidence in God's grace. It is so sure and certain that a man could stake his life on it a thousand times." Bottom line for Luther was indeed *sola fide*— "The just shall live by faith *alone!*"

Free to Love

What does that have to do with freedom? Everything! When, through the gift of faith, we claim our righteousness with God, we know with assurance that we are loved and that nothing can change that. The insecurity of having to be adequate is gone. We are free to be ourselves, love ourselves, and give ourselves away to others. When we know that God is pleased with us out of sheer grace we could never deserve, we do not have to try to win His pleasure. The outcome is joy and an unstudied capacity to do those things that are indeed pleasing to Him—not as a requirement, but as a result. The test of freedom is not just what we are free to do, but what we are free not to have to do.

This has amazing implications for our relationships with people in our lives. We are freed from the necessity to earn the love of people and to require that they justify our love for them. Bartered approval is no longer required. When I think of people with whom I am free to be myself, I find without exception that they are people who are so secure in God's unmerited favor that they exude acceptance of me. I feel affirmed and liberated in their presence. The secret is that they feel good about themselves! This has helped me to realize that I imprison people with judgment, guilt, and feelings of inadequacy when I feel badly about myself. The only cure for that is fresh grace.

Most of us establish performance expectations for our relationships. "I will love you if and when—" we say or imply. The cause is usually our own insecure relationship with our Lord. When we are not free in that relationship, there is slim chance that the people around us will be free. Paul Sherer said, "We find freedom when we find God; we lose it when we lose him." The essence of our freedom is that God will never lose us. When that assurance becomes the ever-recurring experience of our faith, we will become free. We need to do as G. K. Chesterton suggested: "Let your religion be less a theory and more a love affair."

Filled with Joy

Joy is the sure sign that the Holy Spirit has taken up residence in us. It is a fruit of the Spirit. Whenever we feel a lack of joy, we need fresh grace. Joy is the direct result of God's love "poured into our hearts by the Holy Spirit who was given to us" (Rom. 5:5).

Luke gives us a startling account of the joy of the early Christians at the end of Acts 13. He sandwiches an amazing statement between two experiences of difficulty, rejection, and persecution: "And the disciples were filled with joy and with the Holy Spirit" (vs. 52).

Joy is always the result of God's freeing grace in our lives. The greatest discovery that I have made in the midst of all the difficulties of life is that I can have joy when I don't feel like it. When I had every reason to feel beaten, I felt joy. In spite of everything, the Holy Spirit has given me the conviction of being loved and the certainty that nothing could separate me from Him. Joy is a fruit, a manifestation of the indwelling Holy Spirit in our lives.

We can't help marveling at Paul and his friends. In both Antioch and Iconium they poured out their lives for people. They preached, taught, and ministered with love. Their success always elicited renewed rage from many of the Jews. The temptation to give up could have engulfed the apostles if it were not for the power of the Holy Spirit. They did not view difficulties as a sign of defeat, but as a call to the next place to share love.

That's the mood I sense in Paul and his followers. They had done all they could. The world was waiting for the gospel. Antioch was in the Lord's hands. The preaching of the gospel had taken root, and the city would never hear the end of it! No wonder the winsome evangelists were filled with joy and the Holy Spirit. Confident trust burst forth in joy.

But there are deeper reasons for this joy. Based on the whole witness of the New Testament, we can surmise the source of the joy engendered by the Holy Spirit: the Lord Jesus Himself. He is synonymous with joy. At his nativity the angels proclaimed, "I am bringing you good news of great joy for all the people" (Luke 2:10). Joy was the exclamation point of his message, "I have said these things to you so that my joy may be in you, and that your joy may be complete" (John 15:11). Jesus' resurrection victory brought joy. If death could be defeated, all things were possible.

There is another reason for the joy of Paul and his band. Joy is not only an outer expression of the inner work of grace in our hearts; it's an expression of delight over being part of the transformation of the world. The evangelists had been a part of the miraculous transformation of hundreds of people who had given their lives to Christ. There is no greater joy. If we are not involved in personal caring to help others know Christ, our own personal concerns will sink us. To miss the joy of caring for others is to miss everything.

Finally, their fellowship together was a joy. They had each other. I like to imagine what they said to each other after each traumatic difficulty. I can feel the encouragement that they gave each other as they bound up each other's wounds, "I couldn't have made it without you." More than fighting a common enemy, they shared a common cause nourished by an undiminishable conviction.

We all need the joy of fellowship. We were never meant to make it alone. Our Lord uses the difficult times to break us open to a receptive dependence on our brothers and sisters in faith. We need them to remind us of our real purpose and of our only source of power.

In the Senate, there are numerous small groups for Bible study and prayer besides the senators' Bible study group. These are tremendous sources of strength and courage for the participants. Senators, senators' spouses, and staff members can come to these meetings filled with hope and hurt and leave with the mutual support of prayer. For example, a small group of senators meets nearly every day for a brief time of sharing needs and prayer with one another. One senator told me, "I go to the meeting weighted down; I leave feeling fresh freedom from the Lord."

Paul's stirring message of freedom in Christ won him a hearing from the whole city of Antioch. Some of the Jews who had been profoundly moved by him in the synagogue became deeply disturbed by the positive response from the city's Gentiles. Many were filled with jealousy. But the Gentiles' positive response confirmed the guidance of the Holy Spirit in Paul's life: He was to go to the Gentiles. The Gentiles were responsive even though many of the Jews persistently dogged Paul's tracks, disturbing his ministry and dissuading converts. But freedom in Christ provided joy in the midst of this persecution, "and the word of the Lord spread throughout all the region."

Where do you need joy in your life? Check the inflow of grace in that relationship or responsibility. Dare to pray for fresh grace. Joy will be a direct result.

10
Idols of the Heart

Acts 14:8-28

I once was invited to preach at a church that had an interesting neon sign on the roof. The bright letters spelled out "JESUS ONLY!" My homiletical mind darted to different ways I could finish that sentence: Jesus only saves; Jesus only sustains; Jesus only strengthens; Jesus only secures. Not a bad claim for a church.

I discovered that the sign had been erected years before. It was put there to declare to the world that this was one church that would depend on Christ alone. But now, by the people's own admission, the words have been changed to read "JESUS AND!"

These people believed in Christ, but as for many contemporary Christians, He had become just one of the many sources of security, meaning, and purpose. Their daily lives contradicted the sign. Family, jobs, possessions, people, achievements of the past, hopes for the future and for the nation—all ranked closely with Jesus in the raw pressures of life. The church members really wanted the sign to be true; so do I. But to make it true, Jesus had to become more than one of many gods.

Syncretism—the spiritual sickness of having more than one god— has been around for a long time. It never troubled the ancient Greeks very much. They had a pantheon of gods, and there was always room for one more. The people of Israel constantly were tempted to add the fertility or war gods of pagan nations to Yahweh for good measure. The prophet Elijah almost lost his life by confronting that enfeebling dilution. His words are strangely penetrating even today for Christians in the Church: "How long will you go limping with two different opinions? If the Lord is God, follow him; but if Baal, then follow him" (1 Kings 18:21). It ultimately comes down to that choice, doesn't it?

The Lord later called Ezekiel to deliver a similar message to the Jews in exile:

> These men have set up idols in their hearts, and put before them that which causes them to stumble into iniquity. . . . Therefore speak to them, and say to them, 'Thus says the Lord GOD: "Everyone of the house of Israel who sets up his idols in his heart, and puts before him what causes him to stumble into iniquity, and then comes to the prophet, I the LORD will answer him who comes, according to the multitude of his idols, that I may seize the house of Israel by their heart, because they are all estranged from me by their idols."' (Ezekiel 14:3-5, NKJV)

The Lord will accept anything in us except a place in our constellation of diminutive gods. The ultimate manipulation of Christ is the idolatry of people and things, putting them on an equal status with Him.

Gods or Mortals?

This was exactly what Paul and Barnabas faced in the city of Lystra. Before coming there, they had survived hostility, hatred, persecution, and near-death because of the gospel. They had experienced every possible response to Christ from Jew and Gentile alike. But the response of the people of Lystra to their message was something altogether different.

I want to focus our exposition in this chapter on the ending of Paul's first missionary journey recorded in Acts 14. The Lystra experience has implications for us today. Lystra was about six hours' journey, by foot, southwest from the city of Iconium, where Paul and Barnabas had joyfully endured resistance and persecution. In most places the Gentiles heard them gladly. At Lystra they heard them all too gladly.

I came across an ancient myth by Ovid, the Roman poet, that helps explain the people's quickness to receive these missionaries. The legend says that the gods Zeus and Hermes had come to that region disguised as mortals. No one accepted or welcomed them except one couple, Philemon and Baucis. A flood of judgment was sent in retaliation, and all were drowned except this old couple. They were made guardians of a spectacular temple outside of Lystra and were turned into great, magnificent trees when they died. Familiar with this folk legend, the people of Lystra were taking no chances. They welcomed Paul and Barnabas and gave them access to their city. They watched them carefully. Could this be Zeus and Hermes returned a second time?

Obviously the two apostles did not realize that they were being sized up for deification. They immediately went about their usual activities of preaching and teaching Christ. We are sure they proclaimed Christ at the beginning of their ministry because of the manifestation of faith in a man who was crippled from birth. Only Christ enables the kind of faith Paul observed in the man's face as he preached: "He listened to Paul speaking; and Paul, looking intently at him and seeing that he had faith to be made well, said in a loud voice, 'Stand upright on your feet!' And he sprang up and walked" (Acts 14:9-10). The cripple was healed.

That did it! Now the people were convinced that Zeus and Hermes had returned. But they had been so intent on fitting Paul and Barnabas into the personified categories of their previously established deities that they did not hear what the apostles said about Christ and His salvation. They were so excited that they lapsed from Greek into their native Lycaonian as rumors reached a fervor: "The gods have come down to us in human form!" they shouted. Barnabas, massive and strong of stature, they identified as Zeus, the head of the ancient Greek pantheon; and Paul, because of his gift of speech, they called Hermes, the god distinguished for eloquence and rhetoric. The celebrative excitement of the crowd grew as they devised ways of welcoming their "gods." Just outside the city gate stood the temple

memorializing the previously inhospitable reception of these very
gods. The people would spare nothing this time! Oxen were prepared
for sacrifice; garlands of flowers were draped over the sacrificial oxen
and on the visiting deities and spread everywhere in honor of
their coming.

Only One God

It finally dawned on Paul and Barnabas what was happening. The
people had not heard the gospel they preached. Instead, the two of
them were about to be deified in the Greek pantheon. Horror gripped
them. What could they do? How could they make the people understand that they had come to Lystra not to be made great but to
preach a great Christ; not to become two of many gods, but to proclaim the living God?

The apostles tore their garments—not a very godlike thing to do.
But that was a radical Hebrew way of expressing consternation over
a sacrilege. The high priest had done this with angered rage over
Jesus. Now, in a strange twist, here were two followers of Jesus rend-
ing their clothes in a desperate attempt to acknowledge Christ as
Lord, and not become counterfeit gods themselves. Something had
to be done and said to help the people understand that they were
men—human beings—just like themselves, in need of the true God
as much as they were.

We think of the many great politicians, monarchs, generals, and
preachers who have failed at just that point. History's pages are filled
with accounts of gifted leaders who have manipulated the populace
to follow them as deified answers to people's need to be led. Most of
them have ended up being manipulated by the very mobs they created.

Paul refused to be one of Lystra's gods. "Friends, why are you
doing this?" he asked. "We are mortals just like you, and we bring
you good news, that you should turn from these worthless things to
the living God" (vs. 15). He wanted the people to know that he had
the same weaknesses, inadequacies, and appetites they had. He had
tried his own variety of vain and worthless efforts to justify himself
before gods of his own making. Here is an incisive word for the
Christian communicator and witness. What God has done with the

raw material of our human natures makes our message compelling and believable. We are not here to impress people with piety, but to present our impressive Christ, who deals with our spiritual poverty.

Paul showed his skill at communication. He began where the people were, with what they believed. His purpose was to proclaim one God who is Lord, Creator, and source of all. He began with the known realities of the heaven, earth, and sea; the seasons, rains, and harvest; the benevolent providence of food and gladness. From these taken-for-granted blessings, he revealed their source in the Lord God of all creation.

But still the people did not listen. Paul's eloquence, and not what he said, fortified their determination to honor him as one of their gods. (The most effective way of evading truth is to deal with it rather than having it deal with us.) They cheered Paul as Hermes and refused to come to grips with the true God he proclaimed. They did not really want to learn what their new "god" said; they wanted him on their own terms. By their accolades they kept him from going on to present the truth that the only true God had humbly come "in the likeness of man" to live and die for their salvation. Sentimentalism kept them from salvation!

The Ultimate Manipulation

I am prompted to make a comparison of Christians in America today with the people of Lystra. Most of us have come to Christ with carefully set securities. We accept Him as Savior out of our need for further security, assurance of His love for daily pressures and promise of eternal life. Like the people of Lystra, we keep our other gods. Idolatry of Christ as a historical figure makes us fanatics about the celebration of His birth and death. But idolatry is always adoration at a distance. It's the ultimate manipulation. We get what we want and need, but *avoid the penetrating transformation of our lives.* We whittle Christ down to our size and fit Him into the portfolios holding our accumulation of gods.

There is no more clever way of capturing and domesticating truth than accepting it and rehoning it to fit our preciously held ideas and convictions. We do that with Christ all the time. We all have needs for strength and power to do and be what we have envisioned. We all long for wisdom and insight, effectiveness and influence. Christ can provide that. So we accept Him and His love to enable us to get on with our predetermined goals. By our worship and adoration, we avoid the radical reorientation of our natures and the direction of our lives.

All too often today, Jesus is treated like a V.I.P. to be honored, but not believed in or followed. In America, He has become a custom but not the true Christ; a captured hero of a casual civil religion, but not the Lord of our lives. We have never really grappled with the question asked at His birth, "What shall we do with the child who is born?" Or during His ministry, "What can we do with this Jesus who claims to be the Christ?" Or Pilate's mocking question to the Jews in the mob at Jesus' trial before His death, "Then what do you wish me to do with the man you call the King of the Jews?" (Mark 15:12).

After the Crucifixion and Resurrection the question was not silenced. It became focused on the people in whom the living Christ reigned: "What shall we do with these men?" (vs.16). The people in Lystra answered that question most cleverly of all. And as in Lystra, our times have answered with equal evasion and equivocation. "Take Him in! Accept Jesus as the greatest man who ever lived! Revere Him as the most penetrating psychologist who ever analyzed life. Mark the calendar B.C. and A.D. Plan your customs around His birth, death, and Resurrection. Speak of the gentle Jesus, meek and mild. Paint portraits of Him, write the libraries full of line and verse about Him. Sing for Him; preach about Him." We have done everything we can with human skill and duration except one—*made Him the absolute Lord of our lives!*

We have almost been successful at making Christ fit our specifications. We have tried to do what people attempted during the Savior's earthly ministry. The disciples and the leaders of Israel all tried it. But He would not be manipulated. Nor will He be now. He wants nothing less than to have us become new creatures in Him. He must become the only Lord of our lives, the only guide of our activities. Then the labyrinth of secondary, falsely deified diminutive gods can be put into perspective. Then the pantheon of gods in our security system—people, position, possessions, and plans—can become expressions of our loyalty to Christ and dependence on Him. Hymn writer Isaac Watts expresses what we owe to the Lord of our lives:

> When I survey the wondrous cross
>   On which the Prince of Glory died,
> My richest gain I count but loss,
>   And pour contempt on all my pride.
>
> Were the whole realm of nature mine,
>   That were a present far too small;
> Love so amazing, so divine,
>   Demands my soul, my life, my all.

Honoring the Messenger Instead of the Message

There's another aspect of the Lystra story that exposes our effort to dilute and manipulate the truth. We put the communicator on a pedestal and ignore the communication. We have a seemingly limitless capacity to give the honor that belongs to Christ to the people who seek to introduce us to Him. Pastors, parents, friends, and teachers who have brought us the good news are often made the source of our security. We elevate them to supersainthood and miss for ourselves the dynamic that has made them admirable. We make matinee idols out of Christian leaders and forget that the greatest honor we can pay them is to become what we admire in them. There is no finer affirmation than to live the faith they have exemplified. The reason there are so many prima donnas in the pulpit is that we have given the messenger more honor than the message. We need someone to be for us what we are not willing to become ourselves.

Paul learned what every Christian leader is eventually forced to discover: there is no rage like that of a rejected manipulator. If that person cannot fit Christ or His spokesman into a comfortable compartment that suits his or her own ends, that person will turn in angry retribution.

I talked to a church officer from a congregation whose pastor had resigned under conflict. I asked the man what happened. "The pastor

did not fit," he said. "He preached a Christ that rocked our founda-
tions. Everything that we hold dear in our traditions came into question. He did not help us to live our lives; he made us question all
our beliefs. The people could not take it. Besides that, he told us
about his own needs to grow in Christ. How can a person who has
needs help us with our needs?" I could hardly believe what I heard.
The man did not realize the self-incrimination in his own words.
Neither Jesus nor Paul could have pastored his church. They would
not have "fit" either.

Notice how quickly the crowd at Lystra changed. It's rather em-
barrassing to plan a sacrifice and an exalted celebration and have the
guests of honor, visiting "gods" at that, refuse the throne of deification. The excitement over Paul-made-Hermes turned to bitter hatred.
When he would not do what they wanted, they did to him what
people have done for centuries to the gods of their own making who
will not perform to specification: they tried to kill him.

Idolatry usually has a tragic end. Look at the state of Lystra after
the initial preaching of the gospel: the pantheon of pagan gods still
intact; the preachers of the gospel captured as two more gods; and
the people unenlightened. The people were still in charge. Paul was
bitterly stoned by the mob at Lystra under the careful instigation
and instructions of the angry Jews. They left him on a garbage heap
outside the city, thinking he was dead.

God's Surprises
Luke then says, "But when the disciples surrounded him, he got up
and went into the city." What disciples? Did they come from other
communities to assist Paul and Barnabas and to offset the hostile
influence of the Jews who tracked his steps? Perhaps. But further
study reveals that the preaching of the gospel in Lystra had more
results than just the idolatry of the mob.

Two women, Lois and Eunice, had been converted during Paul's
visit there. The grandson of Lois and son of Eunice, young Timothy,
must have made his first commitment to Christ during these stormy
days of Paul's preaching the gospel at Lystra. Timothy later became
Paul's beloved student and disciple. We wonder if he was in that

circle of believers who gathered around Paul to pray.

We do know that their prayers were answered. Paul was not dead! The Lord healed the gouges and blows from the stones. He had promised Paul that he would never be without two strengthening realities: the *Holy Spirit* and the *fellowship of the Church*. What do any of us need more than that? God's surprises are readily available when our ultimate trust is in Him and nothing else!

Paul got back to what he had started at Lystra. He faced the people with the truth they previously refused to consider. Once again Paul became the message he proclaimed. Let your imagination run freely to consider what it must have been like to have the same man they had left for dead come striding back into the city to preach the gospel. No wonder so many became believers. And he would be coming back to encourage and enable them. A strong, vital church would be waiting for him when he returned on his second missionary journey.

We can feel the spring in their steps, the lilt in their voices, and the determination on their faces as Paul and Barnabas finished the first missionary journey in Derbe, went back through the cities where they had preached, and then crossed the sea to Antioch in Syria to share the good news. "When they arrived, they called the church together and related all that God had done with them, and how he had opened a door of faith for the Gentiles" (vs. 27).

What idols of the heart dilute your commitment to Christ? Take some time now to prayerfully ask the Holy Spirit what idols may be syncretized with the Lord in your heart. Success in your profession, the people of your life, the possessions you've accumulated, the popularity you work hard to assure, the position or status you've achieved? It's not easy to become a disciple in our pluralistic society. The only way to survive is to use all you have and all you are to glorify the Lord and not yourself or whatever idol competes with Him in your heart. Then you can say with William Cowper:

> The dearest idol I have known,
> Whate'er that idol be,
> Help me to tear it from Thy throne,
> And worship only Thee.

11
Surprised by the Spirit

Acts 16:6-10

On a grim, foggy winter's day in 1754 at Strawberry Hill, Twickenham, England, Horace Walpole read a Persian fairy tale that brought springtime joy into his life. To share the liberating truth he had just discovered, he wrote a letter to his old friend Horace Mann, who was serving as an envoy to Florence, Italy. In the letter he disclosed the "thrilling approach to life" the folktale had given him and how it had helped him recapture an expectant excitement about his daily work.

The tale described three princes of Ceylon, who had set out in search of great treasures. Though they did not find the treasure for which they searched, they were constantly surprised by more magnificent treasures they had not anticipated. While looking for one thing, they found unexpected delights along the way. During the journey they grew in the realization that the true secret of an adventuresome life is an awareness of unexpected happenings in usual circumstances.

The ancient name of the island of Ceylon is Serendip, which accounts for the title of the fascinating story—"The Three Princes of Serendip." From this, Walpole coined the word *serendipity* to explain a reality that he had learned through studies and work. The most significant and valued experiences happen when you are least expecting them, and the serendipity always becomes more precious than the thing sought.

Seren-dip-ity. The parts of the word unlock its meaning: the dip of the serene into the secular, into this age and time. For the Christian, it is the breakthrough of the Holy Spirit into our usual circumstances, the surprise that comes to us when we are seeking to know and do His will.

Marks of Supernatural Living

A life lived freely in the Spirit is distinguished by *surprisability*. An eighth beatitude might be, "Blessed are those who are surprisable, for the unexpected always happens." When we lose our capacity to be surprisable, we settle into a rut of responsibilities and demands with the terrible conviction that we must do everything ourselves. We expect very little and are not disappointed; we aim at nothing and we hit it. One thing I know about God: He delights in surprising us with solutions we never expected.

A Spirit-led life is expressed in *spontaneity*. It is the capacity to grasp the unexpected, the freedom to respond to the unplanned. A tragic thing happens to us when we outplan God and resist His interventions because they were not on our carefully calculated agendas.

An openness to unscheduled gifts results in supernatural *sagacity*. The Holy Spirit infuses us with penetrating insight, sound judgment, and keen perception. These are intellectual surprises of wisdom. Our lives are marked by serendipitous wisdom when we suddenly see answers and directions we had not anticipated. We are inspired by insight from beyond. It's the grand realization, "Well, I had never thought of that!"

Sensitivity to life and people is the result. We come to know what Elizabeth Barrett Browning meant:

> Earth's crammed with heaven,
>   And every common bush afire with God;
> But only he who sees, takes off his shoes.

Led by the Spirit, we come alive to unlimited possibilities. Every person and situation becomes a gift crammed with God. We discover that the process is as important as the product and that people are the valued discoveries of the process. People themselves, as unique gifts, become God's serendipities.

The crowning joy of this spontaneous life is *security*. We come to expect great things from God and are free therefore to dare great things for Him. Eventually we come to expect surprises and learn that God will always be on time with His gracious, liberating infusion of power and direction. When we get to the place where our lives are completely under His control and our decisions are guided by expectant prayer, we become profoundly secure in the reliability of His providence. Instead of saying with Jacob, "The Lord is in this place and I knew it not," our fellowship with the ubiquitous Holy Spirit, our ever-present Friend, causes us to say, "The Lord is in this place, and we know it!"

Unexpected Guidance

Acts 16:6-10 presents us with Luke's description of living a life open to God's surprises. We find Paul, Silas, and the newly recruited Timothy on the next lap of the second missionary journey in search of new converts to Christ in Pamphylia and regions beyond. Like the princes of Serendip, the three adventurers in Christ headed out toward new frontiers to conquer and were surprised by an unexpected blessing they could never have planned or anticipated.

Paul wanted to go to the Roman province of Asia (not to be confused with what we think of today as Asia, but the adjoining province west of Pamphylia extending over to the eastern coast of the Aegean Sea). He felt that this should be the next focus of the Spirit's strategy. However, the Holy Spirit said no. Luke's language describing the closed door on the province of Asia is very specific: ". . . having been forbidden by the Holy Spirit to speak the word in Asia" (Acts 16:6). The Greek word for *forbidden* is *kōluthentes*, the aorist past participle form of *kōluō*, meaning "to hinder." It expresses antecedent action; that is, prior to entering Asia, the Holy Spirit made it clear that Asia was not a priority.

How this was expressed we do not know. Some have suggested

that sickness prevented Paul's going. Others have conjectured that resistance from the Jews made the journey untenable. Still others have supposed direct, forbidding guidance from the Holy Spirit. Whether the Holy Spirit said no in inner feeling or outer frustration, the result was the same. Paul was a Spirit-sensitized man who could read the signposts erected for his direction. I prefer to believe that this prayer-saturated saint was so open to guidance that the Spirit could implant convictions of direction in his mind and heart. The Lord had something greater in mind than the sought-for treasure in Asia.

With the door of Asia slammed shut by the Holy Spirit, the three princes of the King headed north to preach throughout Phrygian and Galatian territory. Unanticipated surprises occurred all along the way. People found new life in the Savior and new churches were born. Paul's letter to the Galatians helps us appreciate the extent of this phase of the mission. But the greatest surprise God had prepared was still ahead.

Further north, the adventuresome band approached the border of Mysia. When they came opposite Mysia, they wanted to go northeast to the wilderness area of Bithynia. Luke tells us that the "Spirit of Jesus did not allow them" (vs. 7). Here the Greek verb used is a present active form, which means that, whereas the first prohibition was prior, this one was simultaneous. Paul and his companions wanted to go in one direction. The Lord wanted them to go in just the opposite direction. With another door closed, they headed east to Troas on the Aegean coast.

More Than a Dream

The supreme supernatural intervention of the Lord took place there, given to Paul in a dream. A man from Macedonia across the sea appeared in the dream with this compelling supplication, "Come over to Macedonia and help us" (vs. 9). When the apostle awoke, he knew his uncertain wandering was over. Here was a clear direction. He and his friends would go over to Macedonia to preach the gospel there.

The Acts account becomes first person at this point. This is the first of the "we" passages, indicating that it was at Troas that Luke himself joined Paul and his band. Some questions arise about Luke's influence on Paul's serendipitous dream. Was Luke from Macedonia? Was he the personification in the dream? Or had Paul, Luke, and the others talked to a Macedonian about the territory's need for the gospel on the day before the guiding dream occurred?

We do not know. What we do know is that the term Luke uses to describe the nature of the Lord's guidance indicates that perhaps reason and revelation had coalesced to make the direction indubitably clear. "And when he [Paul] had seen the vision, immediately we sought to cross over to Macedonia, concluding that the Lord had called us to preach the gospel to them" (vs. 10, NKJV). The word for "concluding" is *sunbibazontes*, the present active participle of *sunbibazō*, meaning "to go together, to coalesce, to bind or knit together, to make things agree and arrive at a conclusion." That strongly suggests that the vision substantiated a prior possibility. Perhaps Luke and Paul had discussed what God was saying to each of them. He had brought them together in this seaport. They must have wondered: "Lord what are You trying to tell us? Why the closed doors? What next? Where do You want us to go according to Your infinite wisdom and infallible strategy? Macedonia?"

The dream removed all doubts. It radically altered and immeasurably released the Church to change the world. The spread of the Church to Europe and eventually the world mission of the Church resulted from the serendipitous intervention of God at Troas. G. Campbell Morgan affirms this in his commentary *The Acts of the Apostles:* "It is better to go to Troas with God than anywhere else without him." Because Paul went to Troas with God, he could now bring God's good news to Europe. In search of one treasure in Asia, he discovered an infinitely greater one along the way.

The River of the Spirit
This penetrating paragraph of Acts has deepened our understanding of the ways the Spirit can break into our daily lives.

First of all, the truly Spirit-sensitive life surfaces in the stream of the Holy Spirit. Paul had been caught up in the fast-moving currents of the Spirit's movement in history. Immersion in the Spirit's presence gave him guidance and enabled him to make right decisions.

Guidance is not something we go to God to get; it is the inner assurance that comes from being carried along the riverbed, through the rocks and rapids of dangerous alternatives. In Psalm 46:4 we see the promise that is realized in post-Pentecost power, "There is a river whose streams make glad the city of God, the holy habitation of the Most High."

To me, that means God's presence among us will be like a flowing river. The "Most High" knows the past, present, and future, beyond time and space; yet He has chosen to flow in human affairs to guide and direct our decisions according to His infinite wisdom.

This same image is found in Isaiah's prophecy, which we now see fulfilled in Christ and experience through His Spirit:

> I am about to do a new thing;
>   now it springs forth; do you not perceive it?
> I will make a way in the wilderness
>   and rivers in the desert. (43:19)

Catch the undeniable relationship of the river and the outpouring of the Spirit in Isaiah 44:3:

> For I will pour water on the thirsty land,
>   and streams on the dry ground;
> I will pour my Spirit upon your descendants,
>   and my blessing on your offspring.

John, too, caught the vision of the river of God's Spirit, "Then the angel showed me the river of the water of life, bright as crystal, flowing from the throne of God and of the Lamb" (Rev. 22:1). Paul and his missionary friends were being carried by the river of the Holy Spirit. They had stepped into the fast-moving currents of the Lord's guidance. They were not so much seeking guidance as they were caught in a flow of guidance. With each decision, they were swept along, given instructions and directions before and in the midst of each phase of the evolving mission. The Holy Spirit was constant and consistent.

God's No Becomes Yes

The second thing this passage has taught me is that in the flow of the Spirit, the Lord's no becomes part of His ultimate yes! As we are carried along in the stream of the Spirit, we can depend on both our reason and our inner feelings. We belong to our Lord. If we have surrendered all of life to Him, we can dare to trust our negative as well as positive thoughts and feelings. There are certain possibilities that are not right for us if we want to be available for what God has planned.

It was not the Lord's timing for Paul to go into the Roman province of Asia at that time, although later it would be right for him to go to Ephesus on the coast of that province. The Lycus valley of the region would never be touched by Paul personally. Colossae, Laodicea, and the other cities of the area would be reached later by his disciple Epaphras and would be entrusted by the Lord to the faithful pastoral care of the apostle John. Both Revelation and the pastoral epistles of John give us evidence that the Lord took care of that area in His own way and according to His own strategy. Master Strategist and Planner, God had more than the apostle Paul to deploy. He gave His no to Paul about going into Asia because He wanted to get him on to Macedonia. Retrospectively, we can see that He was right.

We all know times when we feel blocked and certain directions seem to be wrong. The temptation is to get out of the flow of the river and move up some little stream of our own choosing. Sometimes, when we do, being cut off from the Spirit's guidance results in depleted energies and ineffectiveness in our efforts. Often, it takes the Lord a long time to get us back into the mainstream, out of the eddies of our own self-determinism. Paul could have gotten stuck in Asia, never to be heard of again, unless the current of the Holy Spirit had torn loose Paul's tenacious efforts to rechannel the riverbed the Spirit was cutting through the wilderness ahead of him.

While canoing in the wilds years ago, I recall the seasoned instructions of our Canadian guide who told me how to keep my directions clear and not get lost. He said, "Stay in the main river. Let it carry you south. Don't get off into side streams that only appear to be the way to go, or you'll never make it." Sound advice for life in the Spirit as well!

I am alarmed by some of the things I have almost done in my life. Looking back, they would have been disastrous for the ultimate life God wanted me to live. In times like that, the drumbeat of the Master becomes quiet and then stops altogether. Awesome inner silence! In its deafening quiet I have heard God's undeniable *no*. When I resolve *not to do* what seemed so right by my own standards of judgment, God's drumbeat begins again, quickening its pace as I turn in a new direction.

The Risk of Obedience

Going in the direction that is guided always involves risk. That's the third thing this passage reveals. Paul and his band pressed on, taking the risk that the Holy Spirit knew what He was doing with them. When they were forbidden by the Spirit to go into Asia or Mysia, they did not make camp and refuse to proceed. They risked moving in new directions each time the road they were on was disqualified by the intervening Lord. These actions led them to Troas and to an assurance of what they were to do.

I must confess that I don't enjoy ambiguity. There are times I wish the Lord would write out the instructions and send them by some angelic messenger so that I would *know* what I should do and say for every moment of the rest of my life. But the Lord knows me too well to do that! He knows that I would put my trust in the instructions and not in daily, momentary communication with Him.

He gives me the long-range goals, to be sure. I am not in doubt about the central purpose of my life to proclaim the gospel, communicate love to individuals, and become part of the adventure of the Church. But for the daily decisions about priorities and programs, He gives only as much as I need to know in order to do His will in each situation.

The risk is daring to believe that He will be faithful and give me all I need to know, say, and do in each challenge and opportunity. That way I can learn from both the failures and successes. When I offer the Holy Spirit a ready and eager mind, an alert and aware sensitivity, and live in consistent communication with Him, He gives me discernment. The author of Proverbs knew this:

> Trust in the Lord with all your heart,
>   and do not rely on your own insight.
> In all your ways acknowledge him,
>   and he will make straight your paths. (3:5-6)

Along the path, there will be surprises we never anticipated. Our assurance is that God knows what He is doing. He can and will get through to us with His plan. Our willingness makes possible His wonders, and He will use our obedience to generate productivity we never imagined possible. That's the wonder and excitement of Holy Spirit living.

12

Turning the World Right Side Up

Acts 16:11–17:34

An old Gaelic benediction expresses hope and supernatural strength: "May the wind always be at your back." This turned out to be true for Paul. When he and his adventuresome missionary band set sail for Macedonia with a clear and decisive call from the Lord, Luke tells us in Acts 16:11 that they took "a straight course" (a "direct voyage" in the Revised Standard Version). He uses a Greek nautical term for sailing "in front of the wind," giving the idea of the sea pressing a vessel on through the sea. That must have been a liberating affirmation for Paul. The wind, and the Holy Spirit, were both pushing Paul to the next phase of God's strategy for expanding the Church.

We feel that same power filling the sails of the apostles all through the Macedonian ministry and beyond into Greece. The Lord stood out front beckoning them, beside them as companion, within them as gift-giving Spirit, and behind them with driving power. Surely this all-encompassing presence of the Spirit is the reason Paul's life in Christ was glorious and yet brought such disturbance wherever he went.

The Uproar in Thessalonica

Paul's travels related in Acts 16:11–17:34 portray a quality of life in Christ that desperately needs to be rediscovered by Christians and the Church today. The key verse expressing this quality comes from an incited mob in Thessalonica. The enraged mob cried, "These people who have been turning the world upside down have come here also" (17:6). Moffatt translates it, "These upsetters of the whole world have come here too." This statement could well have been a motto or mission statement for the amazing New Testament Church. It dramatizes the dynamics of Paul's life and explains the difficulty he had in Thessalonica and in the cities of Philippi and Athens. No communicator ever received a finer compliment. In Philippi, Paul and his people were accused of disturbing the city, and in Athens his teaching brought consternation. What was it that caused such a strong reaction? Whatever it was, we need to recover it today.

I believe the reason for the triumph and trouble in Paul's ministry is that he uncompromisingly preached the essential truth of the gospel: Christ the Messiah—the crucified, resurrected, living Lord of all life. He could not be dissuaded by side issues or distracted by beguiling philosophies. He proclaimed the essentials of new life in Christ, and the necessity of absolute allegiance and obedience. Cutting a swath through the economic, religious, and philosophic presuppositions and loyalties of the time, his message earned him the title of "upsetter of the whole world." Indeed, he was that. So was the Master before him, and so we must be.

The Simple Essentials

I once heard evangelist and missionary E. Stanley Jones say, "Life is awfully simple or simply awful." There is a difference between being simplistic and being profoundly simple. It's one thing to be simplistic because we have not examined alternatives to a truth we hold; it's quite another to be incisively simple because we have studied and sifted through alternatives and have come to a settled conviction of a truth which clarifies and conditions all others. Simplification is the result of penetrating thought and experience, not a substitute. It enables us to cut through complexities with unadorned incisiveness and clarity.

Paul, one of the most brilliant and highly educated men who ever lived, was simple because he was an essentialist. As a scholar he worked his way through all of the philosophies which captured the minds of his time. As a honed Pharisee, he had an impeccable education in religion. As a man, he tried all of the facsimiles for meaning and purpose and found them wanting. His experience of Christ brought integrating unity to his mind and heart. His gifts as an intellectual were captured to think through the implications of Christ as the only Savior and Lord. His sensitive spirit was infused with the unifying power of the indwelling Holy Spirit. Emotional healing and health resulted. His will was marshaled to seek and do the will of his Lord. The result was that he wanted every person to know, experience, and respond to the living Christ. He had no other plan or purpose. That alone was essential for existence.

Christ is the essence of life. Through Him and the power of His Resurrection, men and women can live abundantly, now and forever. Paul's dedication to essentiality would not bend, blend, adjust, or water down this basic message. And that's what got him into trouble.

His message seldom dealt with the cultural or social complexities of the cities in which he preached. But wherever he went, the clear proclamation of the essential gospel cut deeply into social sickness, religious pride, and cultural intellectualism. He did not go about with a self-image of being an upsetter of the world; he preached Christ. The implications of that reorienting dynamic brought confrontation with economic, ecclesiastical, and political injustice resulting in disturbances throughout his ministry and eventually costing him his life.

Back to the Root

Paul would never have thought of himself as a radical, yet he was one of the most radical men of history. He was not a self-appointed revolutionary, yet creative revolution followed wherever he went. Long before the term *radical* took on liberal political overtones, it meant just the opposite. Actually the word means "of the root," pertaining to the original, fundamental, underived essence. Paul was radical in his determination to get to the root of people's need and God's gift of Christ. He plunged through all the layers of distorted thinking and distracting loyalties to the core of people's emptiness and then proclaimed the fullness of the gospel. That action brought a creative revolution—a reordering of priorities, presuppositions, and purposes to conserve the essence of life as God ordained it to be lived.

Paul's Lord was the original creative revolutionary. He called for a radical, to-the-root change and an absolutely new beginning. Jesus demanded repentance, faith, and obedience. The reorienting revolution began in fellowship with Him and emerged in character and conviction. Then in response, His people were challenged to evaluate everything in life and society. The result has always been literally upsetting as people's lives are turned upside down.

The revolution has been going on ever since. For example, the reformers of the sixteenth century had no intention of developing a new or separate Church. They wanted to return to Christ, the essentials of his message, and the model of the New Testament Church. The Scriptures were the mandate of their radical Christianity, which brought revolution in the then indulgence-ridden and politically corrupt Roman Church. New denominations were not the purpose of the reformers. Second- and third-generation organizers of the truth institutionalized into structures and intellectualized into confessions what had begun as an effort to get back to basics.

It's time now to get back to essentials again; to dare to be simple but not simplistic; to order our lives and our churches around Christ and the Scriptures; to allow His lordship to unsettle anything in us or our society that contradicts the gospel. In fact, if what was said of Paul and his men is not being said about us and the churches of which we are a part, there's something wrong. When has anyone said of us that we were turning our world upside down? In the context of that disturbing question, let's look at Luke's account of what happened in the three cities we are considering in this passage.

Economic Interests Upset in Philippi
Philippi was a Roman colony located on the Egnatian Way, the Roman highway that connected the Aegean Sea with the Adriatic. It was occupied by veteran Roman soldiers sent there to colonize it as a reward for years of faithful service to Caesar. Over time the city

had become a little Rome. Roman dress, language, and customs dominated the life of this European city. As an outpost of Rome, its citizens
were given the rights of Roman citizens—autonomous government, and
the same dignity as if they lived in Rome itself. As a result, Philippi
became a leading city with considerable political pride.

Apparently there were few Jews there, because when Paul began
his ministry by the riverbank at what was designated as a Hebrew
place of prayer, he spoke only to women (16:13). It took ten Hebrew
males to establish a synagogue. The anti-Semitic charge subsequently
brought against Paul indicates that Jews were probably not welcome
in Philippi.

Paul initiated his preaching of the gospel in Philippi in a very
benign way. He proclaimed Christ to the Hebrew women, and Lydia
and her whole family became the first fruits of his labors. He could
have gone on like that for a long time without running into trouble,
if it weren't for a slave girl of soothsaying powers. She followed Paul
and his missionary friends wherever they went, saying, "These men
are slaves of the Most High God, who proclaim to you the way of
salvation" (16:17). Quite a compliment!

Yet Paul was annoyed. He knew the difference between the Holy
Spirit's gift of prophecy and the demonic possession that resulted in
fortune-telling. He could easily have accepted the affirmation of Satan
to enable the work of Christ, but as an essentialist he would have
none of it! Actually the girl was deranged, but people with soothsaying gifts were given great honor in those days, since it was believed
that they had lost their wits and that the mind of the gods had been
placed within them. Luke's description of the young woman means
literally that she had "a spirit, a python" (*echousan pneum puthona*).
This superstition derived from the belief that the god Apollo was
embodied in a snake at Delphi, also called Pytho. From that idea,
the name *pytho* was used for anyone in whom the gods were believed
to have implanted unique capacities of soothsaying or ventriloquism.

The truth about her, however, was that she was demon-possessed.
Paul, like his Lord Jesus, was being confronted by the beguiling benediction of Satan on his ministry. He saw the woman for the pitiful
plaything for profit her masters had made her, a person in need of

exorcism and the healing power of the Lord Jesus. To the spirit distorting her he said, "I order you in the name of Jesus Christ to come out of her."

Now Paul was in trouble. He had not come to Philippi to clean up the practice of material gain from human sickness; he simply did what he had to do out of obedience to Christ. Retribution resulted. The owners of the slave girl brought Paul and Silas before the magistrates, charging that they had been disturbing the city, when actually it was these pimps for profit using the demented woman who were disrupting the colony of Rome! We wonder what "front money" they paid the magistrates to buy their favor, for the punishment of Paul and his followers did not fit their "crime." They were severely beaten and placed in stocks in an inner prison.

In the midst of the persecution and imprisonment, Paul returned to essentials. Christ was his faithful Lord. He would intervene. All would be well and used for the glory of God. He and Silas sang hymns at midnight in affirmation of their faith. The Lord's answer was an earthquake, which not only released Paul and Silas and brought about the conversion of the jailer, but also gave birth to a strong Philippian church which would never forget Paul nor the Lord he proclaimed.

The gospel disturbed this city because Paul would not change his message or accept the accolades of demons who used Satan's power to do the Lord's work. Philippi needed to be disturbed. And so does Washington, D.C., or Los Angeles, or New York, or New Orleans, or your city. Preach Christ, live life in Him obediently, refuse a league with satanically induced social problems, and you will have a revolution—be sure of that. The only difference today is that you may find some good church people a part of the embedded society that produces the city's sickness. Then our essentialism will bring us into conflict with more than the magistrates.

Religious Pride Disturbed in Thessalonica

In Thessalonica, where Paul earned the title of an upsetter of the world, he confronted not economic interests, but religious pride. Thessalonica was the capital of Macedonia and a "free city" with its own constitution and magistrates, known as politarchs. It was a flourishing commercial city with an excellent port, and the main street was part of the Roman Egnatian Way. What was to happen to the people there was crucial for the establishment of the Church in Macedonia.

Luke's summary of Paul's ministry in Thessalonica captures the vital elements: the apostle's clear proclamation of the essence of the gospel and the revolution it caused among religious people. Unlike Philippi, Thessalonica had a strong synagogue and a large population of Jews. We are told that Paul focused his ministry among them, proclaiming Christ as the fulfillment of the Scriptures. Note that he did not theorize or philosophize about his ideas. He exposited the Hebrew Scriptures using three methods: argument, explanation, and proof (17:2-3). He wanted to make clear the fundamentals of Jesus as Messiah, His death for the sins of the world, and His Resurrection victory as the only hope. He stated flatly, "This is the Messiah, Jesus whom I am proclaiming to you."

The essentialist was rewarded for his clarity. The gift of faith was given to some of the Jews, a great many of the devout Greeks who had become inquirers on the fringe of the synagogue's life, and some of the leading women of the city. It was the last two categories that got Paul into trouble again. Remember Paul did not go to Thessalonica to cause a revolution in the synagogue. He simply exposited the Scriptures and proclaimed Christ as Savior. That is sure to bring unsettling results in any religious institution.

Some of the Jews were jealous. They had enjoyed the prestige and profit of the proselytes they had brought to Judaism. They neither wanted to accept Paul's teaching nor lose the influence they had gained among the Greeks who did.

What can a religious person do with her or his jealousy of another person who has superior depth and spiritual power? For some, the answer is to demean the person causing the jealousy. The leaders of the synagogue could not admit the real issue, "Look here, our real problem is that our pride has given birth to jealousy. We see a clarity and power in Paul we don't have. He has been able to do for these people what we could not do!"

Because they could not say that, they took the only recourse open to them. They gathered the rabble of the city, fired them into a frenzy of hatred, and sent them to do their dirty work for them. It was the inflamed mob, carefully tutored by the Jewish leaders, who cried out the accusation that was really an affirmation. Paul and Silas had alarmed the city with truth that they knew would be distorted. Indeed, Paul had turned the world upside down. Actually, his gospel was the only hope of setting it right side up!

Again Paul's radical teaching of Christ had exposed the distortions and sickness of the city. The resulting riot was caused not by the gospel but by the vested interests which were upset by it. Paul barely escaped with his life. But as in Philippi, the dynamic seed of the gospel had been planted. A great church resulted and grew strong, later to receive two of Paul's most powerful letters.

Philosophies Turned Upside Down in Athens

Some new disciples guided Paul's journey by sea to Athens. Silas and Luke remained behind to continue the work in Thessalonica. Alone in Athens, Paul continued his indefatigable mission to preach Christ. In this garden of culture, religion, and philosophy, he kept to his essential message. Daily in the agora, the marketplace in the shadow of the magnificent Acropolis, and in the synagogue, his message was the same: "He preached Jesus and the resurrection" (17:18).

This time opposition was to come from a very different source. Here the issue was not economic or religious, but philosophical. Athens had statues for all the gods of their pantheon. Two philosophical schools, however, dominated the city. The devotees of the Epicurean philosophy asserted that happiness and pleasure were the principal aims of life. Everything happened by chance; the gods were remote and did not care, so worry and concern made little difference. Eat, drink, enjoy. The other school, the Stoics, were just the opposite. Everything for them was fated by the gods, and life had to be lived according to nature without emotional intensity or involvement. The purpose of life was to accept nature and find one's place in it. The Stoics were pantheistic, seeing their gods as all and in all.

No wonder the Athenians were upset by Paul's preaching of Christ and the Resurrection. They listened to him and leveled a very serious charge against an intellectual, calling him a "babbler" (17:18). The Greek word means "seed picker," a term used for birds that flit about picking at seeds, or persons who go about scavenging scraps of food. In some cases, it actually meant a philosopher who belonged to no recognized school of thought, but had picked bits and pieces of thought from many different systems of philosophy. The more serious charge against Paul, however, was that he proclaimed foreign deities. His accusers were wrong on both accounts. He was anything but a seed picker gathering up bits of thought. He had one Lord and one central conviction. As for foreign deities, he proclaimed one God and Sovereign of all creation.

The result was that Paul soon had to defend his beliefs before the Areopagus, a kind of philosophical review board that investigated ideas and intellectual persuasions. Eager for argument and debate, the intellectuals of Athens enjoyed disputation of ideas, but always from the safe distance of philosophical contemplation. Luke analyzed the temper of the city: "Now all the Athenians and the foreigners living there would spend their time in nothing but telling or hearing something new" (17:21).

Paul's essentialism about Christ and the Resurrection brought a response, however sophisticated. We are told that the philosophers "took him and brought him to the Areopagus" (17:19). The Greek verb used here is strong, though it does not imply an arrest. They laid hold of Paul with determination, not as violent as the rough provincial magistrates of Philippi or as frenzied as the agitated mob of Thessalonica, but with imperious insistence nonetheless. Paul had upset Athens with his "new" teaching, and the philosophers wanted to hear what he was saying that was causing so much disturbance.

Before the august Areopagus, Paul was a master communicator as he presented the essential message of the gospel. With his unique audience in mind, he used a known idea to explain an unknown idea to them:

Athenians, I see how extremely religious you are in every way. For as I went through the city and looked carefully at the objects of your worship, I found among them an altar with the inscription,

"To an unknown god." What therefore you worship as unknown, this I proclaim to you. (17:22-23)

With that he had the philosophers' attention and he was off with a flourish of impelling rhetoric carefully honed for his listeners.

Paul began with God as Creator, the Source of all life—not the anthropomorphic creation of human speculation, but the Creator of humanity—who designed us to know and love Him. Next Paul proclaimed that God has guided all history and is the One on whom all life depends. God is not the object of human beings' groping search, but human beings are the subject of God's grace. The Spirit then moved Paul into the truth of the Incarnation and forgiveness offered by "a man whom He [God] has appointed." Christ was implied, but the apostle stopped short of proclaiming Christ explicitly because of a further statement he made about Him: ". . . and of this He has given assurance to all by raising Him from the dead" (17:31).

That did it! The idea of the Resurrection brought a heated response from the philosophers. Some mocked Paul, others dismissed him with polite rejection, "We will hear you again about this." We can be sure they had no intention of hearing him again. Any God who raised the dead would require more than philosophical reflection. The Resurrection demanded faith. And what about the One who was raised? The philosophers stopped Paul before he could talk about Him. The Spirit who guided Paul's words was closing in on them, and they wanted nothing of it. They were being pressed beyond the realm of ideas into a confrontation with the living God.

Not All Resist the Gospel

We wonder how Paul would have finished his lecture, which had very subtly become a witness. I am convinced that he would have told the philosophers what repentance and acceptance of Christ could mean to them. But that would have meant a moral inventory, confession, and a decision. Paul did not intentionally stop short of the whole truth; the intimation of his intention made the intellectuals stop him short of the truth, which could have enabled them to live forever. How very sad.

Resistance to the gospel takes many forms. In reality, Athens was no different from Philippi or Thessalonica. In all three cities the pre-eminence of Christ and the power of the Resurrection were rejected. The bland toleration of Athens was no better than the barbarism of the Macedonian frontier.

But Luke had a way of giving a final twist to his vivid accounts. All was not lost in Athens. "Some of them [the Athenians] joined him [Paul] and became believers, including Dionysius the Areopagite and a woman named Damaris, and others with them" (17:34). No little victory. Dionysius was one of the twelve judges of the Areopagus. The historian Eusebius claims that later he became a bishop of the church at Athens and became a martyr for his faith. Damaris was an aristocratic woman of Athens. The "others with them" suggests more than the words would imply to a casual reader. A group of people became a strong church. Paul did not fail in Athens.

Called to Proclaim Christ

Yet Paul's own analysis of his ministry at Athens can be seen in 1 Corinthians 2:1-5. He had gone to Corinth just after Athens, and these verses in his letter to the Corinthians show us his determination to get to the Cross and Christ crucified more quickly and straight-forwardly. The point, however, is that, though Paul felt defeated in Athens, the Holy Spirit was not defeated.

Note that the Spirit allowed Paul to go through the experience of feeling that he had failed. He was pressing the apostle into an even deeper commitment, which he later expressed with new urgency. "When I came to you, brothers and sisters, I did not come proclaiming the mystery of God to you in lofty words or wisdom [as he had in Athens]. For I decided to know nothing among you except Jesus Christ and him crucified" (1 Cor. 2:1-2).

I know how Paul felt and have been forced to learn what he dis-covered. Once I spoke at a college and had little response from the students. I flew home, discouraged by my sense of failure. Where had I missed? I concluded that I had tried to expose *my* learning rather than share what I had learned about the triumphant adequacy of Christ. The experience reminded me about being an essentialist. The

Lord allowed me to live with these feelings for days until His purpose for me became deeply ingrained. Only later did the Spirit allow me the comfort of a flood of letters from students who had indeed found Christ's hope in my speech. I was left with a combination of thanksgiving and a new commitment. It was as if the Lord said, "I used what little you gave Me to work with; what happened is only a portion of what can happen in the future if you will trust Me."

We are called to be upsetters, people who turn the world upside down. To live Christ, share Christ, help people to know Him, and shape our whole lifestyle around Him—that is our only purpose. The world is already upside down in confusion and desperation. When He turns our own world right side up, He calls us to do the same with the world around us. That will require that we become essentialists with one message and a singular hope. And we will never be without the Lord's help to do it.

13
Confident Living

Acts 18:1-23

"I can take anything if I know it will end," a man once told me. "What gets me is when I have a problem like this that won't quit. I don't know how long I can hold out unless I can see the end of the thing!" My friend's difficulty related to living out his faith on his job. He had experienced resistance from his employees and reserve from his supervisors. About the time he thought he had worked out a solution, he received a new blow.

We all feel that way at times. Most of us can empathize, if not with the application of our convictions to our work, certainly in our relationships, challenges, and difficulties in other areas. We can endure brief vicissitudes; it's when they drag on endlessly that we are tempted to give up hope.

Another friend expressed the same feelings about a prolonged illness. "Just when I think I have licked this thing, I have a new setback. Then the demons of despair move in for a frontal attack. I become more sure of the relentless sickness than of God's resources for healing. I don't want to give up, but I'm tempted."

I believe that's the way the apostle Paul felt when he reached Corinth, as recorded in Acts 18. He had been driven out of Macedonia and blandly tolerated in Athens. Persistent hostility from many of the Jews confronted him wherever he went. Would it never stop? Exhausted in body, mind, and spirit, Paul became a prime candidate for despair.

A Discouraged Paul

The ambience of Corinth didn't help much. Sensualism, materialism, and vice confronted him as he finished the fifty-mile walk from Athens and entered the cosmopolitan city. On the rock of Acrocorinth, towering above the city, the temple of Aphrodite reputedly had one thousand consecrated prostitutes. No wonder the term *corinthianize* has become another word for fornication around the world. This boomtown was the capital of the province of Achaia and the chief commercial city of Greece. Voluptuous prosperity mated with frivolous sexuality.

As Paul walked through the marketplace he could see the Arabian balsam, Phoenician dates, Babylonian ivory, Egyptian papyrus, Cilician goats' hair, Lycaonian wool, and Phrygian slaves everywhere for sale in this Vanity Fair of the Roman Empire. What would this pagan city hold for the preaching of the "Life"? The apostle wondered if he had courage to begin again. If he did, how would the people respond? His heart was heavy with memories of Philippi's beating and imprisonment, the Jews' disruption of his success in Berea, the anger of the mob in Thessalonica, the polite, smug complacency of the Athenians. A pall of depression hung over him. Here was a sick, discouraged, troubled man. Later he described his condition in a letter to the church at Corinth: "I came to you in weakness and in fear and in much trembling" (1 Cor. 2:3).

Paul's worst expectations about Corinth were soon confirmed. When he went to the synagogue to proclaim Christ, he met with the opposition he had expected. Many of the Jews reviled him. If he had been rested and refortified, his angry response might have been different. But with the impatience and pique we have when we run out of steam, Paul responded, "Your blood be on your own heads!"—a vitriolic put-down. Then defensively he said, "I am innocent. From now on I will go to the Gentiles" (Acts 18:6). Hurt and hopeless, he implied, "I have tried to share good news with you, and you have shut the door in my face over and over again. Now I'm going to work with people who want to listen."

There were signs of God's providence and intervening care in Corinth, but Paul felt so low he was impervious to them. The Lord gave him friends like Aquila and Priscilla, who came to live in Corinth after they had been driven out of Rome by Claudius. They were fellow tentmakers and believers in Christ as Lord (vss. 2-3). Their hospitality to Paul had helped, but not enough. Crispus, the ruler of the synagogue that had rejected the apostle, became a believer. What more did the troubled Tarsusian want? Some men have preached for years with less response. But, like Elijah of old, this adventurer for the Lord was tired out. The saints of God are most vulnerable when they do their best and evil still seems undefeated.

God's Comforting Words

For the first time, fear dominated Paul's emotions. Like a wounded boxer, he could not make himself get up to face one more punch. More than that, he lost his vision of what God could do in Corinth. But God did not forget his discouraged servant.

The Lord appeared to Paul and said, "Do not be afraid, but speak and do not be silent; for I am with you, and no one will lay a hand on you to harm you, for there are many in this city who are my people" (vss. 9-10). Moffatt translates it thus, "Have no fear, speak on and no one shall attack or injure you; I have many people in this city." The message was clear: "Stop being afraid; speak on no matter how discouraged you are or how filled with doubt or the feeling of ineffectiveness; trust me! I am with you. Proof of that is the people I will give you whom I have elected to be mine."

The Lord says the same thing to you and me. God's words of comfort to Paul can also become our prescription for healing from perplexity and despair. His assurance can replace our attitude of "if anything can go wrong, it will" to the conviction that "if anything can go right, the Lord will make it possible." What a change!

Love Heals Our Fears

The first thing the Lord wanted to heal in Paul and wants to exorcise from us is fear. He wants to lift us out of the syndrome of fearing success because failure may follow. This was a major problem for Paul, who knew that as surely as his ministry was successful there would be conflict with the Jews. It had happened that way wherever he went. I think he got to the place where he was certain that a response from believers would invariably be followed by retaliation. His success always came at a very high personal price. He had been beaten, imprisoned, and rejected. Now he was afraid. He had forgotten that trouble is but the shadow of the wings of the Almighty. He could have used Francis Thompson's perspective from "The Hound of Heaven":

> Is my gloom, after all,
> Shades of His hand, outstretched caressingly?

Paul lost sight of the fact that there was only one man to fear in Corinth: the person who lived in the skin of Saul of Tarsus. It was the inner man the Lord was concerned about. Horizontal tensions were pulling him apart until the vertical Truth pulled him together, saying, "Don't be afraid!"

Paul finally discovered that the Lord will not allow any more difficulty than what will bring a person to deeper faith in Him. Later he wrote to his friends in Corinth: "So far you have faced no trial beyond what man can bear. God keeps faith, and he will not allow you to be tested above your powers, but when the test comes he will at the same time provide a way out, by enabling you to sustain it" (1 Cor. 10:13, NEB). Paul experienced this himself in Corinth.

Fear grips us when we lose our grasp on grace. It is like mist or clouds, which can only be dissipated by sunshine or wind. The warmth of the love of the Son of God and the wind of the Spirit extinguishes the fires of fear. Paul felt newly loved by the Lord. He not only felt loved in a new way through the Master's personal intervention; he also felt new love for the people he feared. We cannot long nurse fear about people we love.

I personally feel Paul was able to praise God for the weakness that had brought him to a new experience of grace. William Law put it this way: "For it is certain that whatever seeming calamity happens

to you, if you thank and praise God for it, you turn it into a blessing."
As I write this, I am encouraged to thank God for the very things
that cause me fear. Perhaps you may be prompted to do the same
thing before going on in this chapter. Another apostle—John—gives
us the hope that experience had carved into his character: "There is
no fear in love, but perfect love casts out fear" (1 John 4:18). Even
now I can feel that healing. Do you?

The Blessing of Weakness

The second ingredient of the Lord's prescription encouraged Paul to
speak and gave him confidence to continue. He learned that weakness
could be a blessing for forceful proclamation. Silence imprisons fear;
boldness liberates it. His own fear, then, was not a curse but a condition for dynamic communication. He would have to depend on
the Lord and not his own eloquence. Paul's uncertainty about his
own gifts not only made him receptive to the gift of the Spirit, but
it also forged a bond of identification with his hearers.

I have learned this repeatedly in my own life. When my strength
is depleted, when my rhetoric is unpolished by human talent, when
I am weary, the Lord has a much better tool for empathetic, sensitive
communication. The barriers are down. When I know I can do nothing by myself, my poverty becomes a channel for His power. Often
when I feel I have been least efficient, people have been helped most
effectively. It's taken me a long time to learn that the lower my
resistance is to the Holy Spirit and the less self-conscious I am, the
more the Word of God comes through. In a time like that, I need
to hear for myself what I am saying more than the listeners; the
result is that they hear what I may have blocked from them before.

What about you? Are you feeling weak or fearful right now?
Thank God! Now's the time to speak and not be silent. It's a blessed
time of productivity—a gift from the Lord. Embrace the troubled
moment; make it a friend. Whatever you do, the glory will go to
Christ and not to you. That's where it belonged all along.

God Is with Us

But we cannot, dare not, speak or move out courageously without the next assurance the Lord gave Paul: "For I am with you" (vs. 10). Many New Testament crises could be punctuated with these words that promise God's abiding presence. To the frightened disciples in Jerusalem at a time of unprecedented uncertainty, He said: "I am with you always" (Matt. 28:20). The Rock of Ages is always the solid foundation with words for the storm: "Come to me, all you who labor and are heavy laden, and I will give you rest" (Matt. 11:28, NKJV). Missionary David Livingstone learned this truth afresh one night in Africa: "I read again that Jesus said, 'Lo, I am with you always.' It's the word of a gentleman and that's the end of it. I will not cross the river by night furtively as I had intended."

The assurance of the Lord's presence is the only way Paul could face Corinth. He could not be in Corinth without being "in Christ." Nor can we live in our cities, jobs, families, churches, or challenges without the confidence of God's "I am with you."

That's the story of the courageous Christians I know about. When the going is rough and they say, "Well, what's going to go wrong next?"—that's when the Voice too deep for words thunders, "I am with you." In this difficult life, seeing "the goodness of the Lord in the land of the living" is often clouded. But God's goodness is all the more ours on this side of Calvary and Pentecost. "Many are the afflictions of the righteous, but the LORD rescues them from them all" (Ps. 34:19). The Living Bible puts it, "The good man does not escape all troubles—he has them too. But the Lord helps him in each and every one." I believe that.

The promise of the Lord's presence is followed quickly in Paul's vision with protecting providence. The Lord assures Paul of help against harm: "No one will lay a hand on you to harm you." That had not always been true: he had known persecution. Nor would it be true in the future: there were physical vicissitudes ahead. The point is that at the moment when Paul could take no more, the Lord interceded for his protection. At future times, when he would be stronger, when what happened could engender deeper faith, and when physical persecution could be used as a witness of his trust and confidence, the Lord would allow it.

It is important for us to remember that the Lord's presence is not a warranty of unlimited protection. We cannot blissfully believe that if we trust in God, life will be a bed of roses. But be sure of this: *He will be with us!* The Lord allows only what we can take. The liberating assurance is that nothing can separate us from Him. With the knowledge that God can use all things for His glory and with the realization that even death cannot defeat us, we can live courageously in the perspective of peace.

The Comfort of Fellowship

The final aspect of the Lord's message to Paul changed his attitude about Corinth and his ministry there. The Lord promised him fellowship to face frustrations. Paul was not alone in Corinth. The Lord said, "There are many in this city who are my people." According to A. T. Robertson's commentary on this passage, some knew they were chosen and called; others would soon be called to faith, if Paul would hold on.

What a refreshing picture it must have been for Paul to know that Corinth was not a foreboding city of hostile people but a city filled with potential converts who would join him in a great Church. I think the Lord wanted to impress two things on the frightened apostle's mind: that Corinth had people who were already alive in the New Life, and that many others were ready to respond. The Lord was saying, "Hang on, Paul! I am at work."

Paul remained unhindered in Corinth eighteen months, preaching and teaching about Christ. He could not have done that without the Lord's recruitment of those He had chosen and elected to believe. They joined the apostle in anticipation rather than anxiety, with expectation rather then mere endurance. Everywhere Paul went, he sought out the Lord's people. No one was excluded from the possibility of becoming a fellow Christian.

Seeing with God's Eyes

Paul's experience in Corinth can happen to all of us in our cities, families, or places of work. We can see with the eyes of the Savior. Then we will see people, not problems; we will discover people who share our vision and who long to find what we have found.

As chaplain of the Senate, I have the privilege of caring for brilliant, highly educated staffers who have come to Washington to work with the senators. Many of them become weary under the heavy load of work and the ups and downs of the political process. For some, being on the "Hill" is a lonely experience. They are tempted to compromise their values. That's why our Wednesday and Friday noon Bible study luncheons have offered fellowship and courage to a number of them. A bright legislative assistant exclaimed, "I'm amazed to find all these believers here! I'm not so alone in my convictions after all."

We have a volunteer chaplain's liaison in every office to keep in touch with people's needs for prayer and support. The Lord has many people all over the Capitol who belong to Him and are discovering they also belong to each other.

When I pastored a church in Hollywood, California, I once talked to an actress who had become a Christian in her last year of graduate training. The warm, loving fellowship there meant a great deal to her emerging life in Christ. When a Hollywood movie company awarded her a contract, she came to Los Angeles wondering if she could ever find the same kind of dynamic friends in Christ she had found in her university. The first months were very disappointing. She concluded that there were no Christians like her in the industry. Temptations to compromise her beliefs and her personal integrity were very disillusioning.

But then someone recommended that she come to see me, and I showed her the Lord's promise to Paul—the Lord had many people in Hollywood too! We prayed that she might receive the ones who were immediately available to help her and others whom the Lord would identify. We prayed that she might find the Lord's people at her studio, apartment building, and social groups. The next day, the Lord gave her several signs of His providence. She dared to be more open to talk about her faith, to "speak and not be silent." Now she is part of a group of movie people seeking to be faithful to Christ and supportive of each other. The Lord changed her attitude about her city and gave her His people.

When a man working in a large company claimed Paul's vision as his own for his corporation, people who shared his need for Christian fellowship suddenly seemed to emerge from the woodwork. Not only that, he became aware of potential Christians all around him who were ready to believe if given a chance. The problem had been his negative view of his surroundings.

Somewhat the same thing happened to a clergyman I met at a conference. Just past middle age and feeling trapped and cornered, he envisioned the rest of his life as one of being occupied with the dreary business of "playing church" with a congregation that seemed unresponsive to the gospel.

After listening intently, I said, "Listen, you don't have to do what you are doing the rest of your life. You're God's person and you'll be a Christian whether you're a clergyman or not. Why not give it your best shot for three more years? Do all the things you have been afraid to try: speak out boldly as if you didn't care whether you succeeded or not; be vulnerable in sharing what the Lord means to you; dare to ask for a band of adventurers out of the congregation to meet with you to discover the Lord's direction. Remember you don't have to stay there forever or be a clergyman the rest of your life. You are free!"

The man's face brightened, he smiled, and then he began to laugh with boyish delight. There were lots of other things he could do, to be sure. He was not trapped after all. The most significant thing about this man's story is that when he returned to his congregation caring so profoundly that he didn't have to care fearfully, he began to model a freedom and abandonment that sparked immediate interest. "What's happened to our pastor?" people asked. One officer remarked, "I've waited all my life to hear someone tell me that what's in the New Testament can be lived now. Our pastor is not only telling about it, he's living it. We can't manipulate him with the usual techniques any more. He's on the move and I want to join him."

Paul found people in Corinth who were the Lord's gift for fellowship, the birth of the Church, protection in difficulties, and the sharing of hope. As we trace his steps through the rest of his ministry, we never again find the fear and frustration he knew before the Corinthian encounter with the Lord. He subsequently faced greater problems and more excruciating persecution, but he never forgot that stimulating vision or ceased to hear the Lord's dynamic promise. Paul was free from fear.

Paul's vision and promise from the Lord are just a prayer away from us. Even if we feel our difficulties are endless and our problems are as sure as the sunrise, the promise can be ours, too. If we give God our fears, He will enable us with grace to love the people and eventualities we fear. We will be able to praise and thank Him for the very things that frighten us. He will show us new ways of speaking about Him from the wells of our weakness. We don't have to be adequate or even strong any more. Our weakness is a gift to expose God's strength. He will not allow any more than we can bear for His glory. And we will not be alone. He will give us people who need Him as much as we do, and who need us. We can live confident, free lives in Christ. People in your city and mine are waiting.

14
Religion Is Not Enough

Acts 18:24–19:7

Someone once asked me what I considered to be the main thrust of my ministry. My answer came quickly, the result of years of thought and experience: "My passion is to introduce people to the living Lord and help them receive His power. There's no limit to what we can do to change the world, share the faith, and help others, if people are filled with the Holy Spirit!"

That statement crystallizes what I have been trying to say in this book: The living, present Holy Spirit replaces the religious chill of distance with the intimacy and intensity of dynamic power. That's why understanding what happened to Apollos and the disciples of John in Ephesus is such a crucial aspect of our study of Acts.

The Ultimate Religious Person
We meet Apollos in the last paragraph of Acts 18. In a few sentences, Luke describes him as a paragon of religious intellect and gives the impressive dimensions of Apollos's dossier. Luke wants us to identify ourselves in the portrait.

First of all, we are told that Apollos was a Jew from Alexandria. If we knew only this, we would still know a great deal, for Alexandria was a great center of learning. It had one of the greatest libraries in antiquity and an outstanding university. The finest learning from both Judaism and Hellenism flowed together in this city of scholars. The wisdom of Plato and Moses met in Alexandria. Greek, Latin, and Hebrew grammar, rhetoric, philosophy, mathematics, medicine, geography, and history filled the atmosphere in which Apollos was raised and educated. As a student of Philo, he probably became skilled in the disciplines of Platonism, Aristotelianism, Stoicism, and Mosaism. If anyone had a right to be intellectually secure and confident, it was Apollos.

But that's only the beginning. Luke goes on to say that Apollos was "an eloquent man" (Acts 18:24). The Greek word for *eloquent* here means to be learned in knowledge and have the ability to express it. He was able to express his thoughts in such a way that he captured the minds and emotions of his listeners. He could marshal words and shades of meaning the same way a skilled conductor of a highly trained orchestra elicits the most subtle nuances of sound.

Apollos was also well versed in Scripture. Not only had he read the accounts of God's actions among his people in what is now our Old Testament, but he was able to interpret them with force and meaning. He followed Philo's allegorical method of scriptural interpretation, finding in each historical account a hidden and deeper meaning. No dry, conceptualist scholar, he could open windows so that his listeners could see through to truth and receive the fresh vitality of his insight. I imagine he knew most of the Old Testament by heart and could make its characters come alive in the mind's eye of his rapt listeners. His interesting and impelling speech won him first a hearing and then a following in Ephesus as people came under the spell of his oratory.

Apollos had experienced the "baptism of John" (vs. 25) and was among the Jewish scholars who were interested in the "Way of God" (vs. 26). His intellectual and spiritual sensitivity made him a ready student of John the Baptist. He could affirm John's preaching of Isaiah, "'Prepare ye the way of the Lord.'. . . Repent and be baptized for the forgiveness of sins." As a spokesman for those who were determined to make way for the Messiah by repentance and purity of life, Apollos had been baptized in an outward sign of absolute abandonment of his life to open the way of the Lord. His Old Testament studies had shown him repeated anticipation of the Messiah and had given him power to prove that Jesus was indeed the Messiah. John the Baptist pointed to the Lamb of God, and Apollos gave Jesus of Nazareth his loyalty and allegiance.

Luke tells us that Apollos could teach "accurately the things concerning Jesus" (vs. 25). He knew about Jesus' life, message, death, and Resurrection. He was fervent in spirit, literally boiling over with emotional enthusiasm. His clear thinking about the Messiah was fueled with intrepid urgency; his convictions could not be deterred. Add to that the courage he showed as he spoke boldly in the synagogue, taking a stand that was very unpopular at this time.

In summary, Apollos was quite a man. He had birth, culture, education under the greatest scholars, intellectual acumen, insight into Scripture, right beliefs, boldness, courage, and convincing communication techniques. But for all his learning and eloquence, Apollos had only the characteristics of John, who baptized with water, without the character of the living Christ, who baptizes with the Holy Spirit. There was religion without release. We could say the same about many churchgoing people today. For them, as for Apollos, there is something missing. Religion is just not enough.

The Missing Dimension

All this background on Apollos prepares us for a most amazing encounter. At the conclusion of one of Apollos's crowd-swaying preaching engagements in the synagogue in Ephesus, two very unlikely people brought creative correction to his life. Filled with the sense of success at the way people had responded, Apollos must have felt the heady wine of adulation.

Then Priscilla and Aquila, two tentmaking friends of the apostle Paul (see Acts 18:1-3), approached Apollos to thank him for his message. They had little in common with him intellectually or culturally, but they shared the belief that Jesus was the Messiah. I imagine that they were able to affirm the young preacher as far as he had gone, complimenting him on his eloquence and knowledge of Scripture. Then I think they became skilled physicians of the Spirit for a gracious but pointed corrective, which must have been very painful. Perhaps they took Apollos to the place where they were lodging so that the great leader would not be embarrassed in front of his avid followers.

Then they shared the missing dimension. Luke says, "they explained to him the way of God more accurately." They told him the exciting news that Jesus was alive as the living, loving, personal, and present Lord in the Holy Spirit. Jesus was not just a fact of history, but a friend of hope. The Christian proclamation no longer signified just the Messiahship of Jesus, but now it included the indwelling power of the Lord. The Christian life meant not just living *for* Christ, but Christ living *in* the believer in the presence of the Holy Spirit—in other words, Pentecost! Bible scholar F. J. Foakes-Jackson observed:

> The teaching of Apollos concerning Jesus, so far as it went, was accurate. But to all appearances the new Christian movement had escaped his notice, and it was certainly late in reaching Alexandria. Aquila and Priscilla heard him in the synagogue and at once realized the power his message would have if only he understood the true significance of what he was endeavoring to teach.

Like the disciples of John whom Paul met later in Ephesus, Apollos probably had to confess, "I have never heard of the Holy Spirit!" What maturity and receptivity Apollos had. He was hungry to learn all that he could. His greatness was not in his previous learning, but in his willingness to learn from two humble, uneducated tentmakers.

If I could give a gift to religious people who do not know God, it would be Apollos's willingness to grow, to see his need, to be viable. He was given the ability to see that his ministry had become self-propelled and self-focused; that people were impressed with Apollos, not the Lord he proclaimed. His listeners were astounded by how he said what he said, not what he said. He was fervent in spirit, rather than filled with the Spirit.

It frightens me to think how easily Apollos could have missed the dynamic of the faith offered to him. He could have said, "Listen, you tentmakers; who are you to tell me how to live or preach! I have gotten along very well up to this time without your help. Look at the excitement of my followers!" Or he could have offered them the familiar con: "Thanks so much for bringing this to my attention. You can be assured that I will give it some thought. Don't call me; I'll call you." Or he could have argued about the facts and missed the personal truth: "How could it be that we have not heard about what happened at Pentecost after the Crucifixion? If it's not known in Alexandria, it's not knowable. Give me proof."

But Apollos had been prepared by the Spirit to receive the missing dimension. Secure in how much he knew, he was open to discover more. He was committed to know all there was to learn about Jesus. What he learned was that the Holy Spirit is Christ alive; what he experienced was Christ indwelling him.

The Signs of the Holy Spirit

What happened to Apollos also happened to the disciples of John the Baptist who we meet in the first paragraph of Acts 19. Apollos and the disciples were of the same breed. Acts 18:24–19:7 must be considered as a whole to catch the full impact of what God wants to give religious people who do not know Him.

I like to think that what happened to the disciples in Ephesus is what our Lord wants to happen in all our churches today. When Paul laid his hands on them, the Holy Spirit came upon them and "they spoke in tongues and prophesied" (19:6). The infusion of the Spirit broke them open at a very deep level to praise God.

The Lord still gives this gift; we all should be open to receive it, but never use it as a lever of judgment on those who have not received it. I have an idea that the religious, uptight disciples of John needed the gift to break free and glorify God with adoration and exultation. As I mentioned earlier, the gift of tongues is not the only undeniable sign that we have received the Holy Spirit. I have never preached that we must seek the gift of "tongues"; rather I have explained that gift of the Spirit without pressure. If God decides to give the gift in order to liberate a person to adore Him, I affirm the gift and press people on to seek even higher gifts as Paul outlined them in 1 Corinthians 12.

The sure sign that people have received the Holy Spirit is love for God expressed in a life of praise and in a desire to communicate what they have found to other people. The gift of prophecy is the sensitive, incisive, and empathetic communication of the implications of the Lordship of Christ in the context of supernatural, Spirit-given insight and wisdom for the unique needs of the people we want to help. When the Holy Spirit is released among people in churches today, there are undeniable signs of love, warmth, and passion to share with people who do not know the Savior, and compassion for the world and its needs.

When Religion Becomes Personal

The inner secret of the change in Apollos is that what he had been preaching became real to him and his own needs. I suggest that he, like so many Christian preachers and writers, had ignored his own message. When Priscilla and Aquila shared what life in Christ was meant to be, only an indwelling Savior could make it possible. Most of us don't need to know how bad we are but, rather, *how great God meant life to be.* That renewed vision necessitates the vitality of the Holy Spirit.

At Corinth in Achaia, Apollos "greatly helped those who through grace had become believers, for he powerfully refuted the Jews in public, showing by the scriptures that the Messiah is Jesus" (18:27-28). Later, in his letter to the Corinthians, Paul affirms the ministry of Apollos in Corinth. "I planted, Apollos watered, but God gave the growth" (1 Cor. 3:6). It is obvious that Apollos became a strong, dynamic leader of the church. He proclaimed more than homilies about the historical Jesus; he offered the infusing, enabling power of an imbuing Savior alive with them. What Jesus had done for His followers in Judea was inseparably related to what He was doing among and within them in Achaia.

The account in Acts of what happened to Apollos when he received power and to the disciples of John when Paul laid hands upon them is an undeniable benchmark for what needs to happen to both the communicators in our churches and the people who listen to them. The difference in Apollos's life after he stopped trying to be self-sufficient and received the Holy Spirit is amazing. As a free person, empowered by God, he was able to build up not Apollos but the Church. Through him, the Lord reached people not with Apollos's adequacy but with the impelling power of the Spirit. The Holy Spirit drives home the gospel, gives the gift of faith to respond, enables acceptance and assurance that spills over to others, and enlists people in the adventure of the movement.

As a pastor and now chaplain of the Senate, I need to live in Apollos's skin and then find myself among the disciples of John in Acts 19. Our problem in the Church today is not that we have never heard of the Holy Spirit, but that we have relegated mention of Him to the repetition of the trinitarian formula, "Father, Son, and Holy Spirit." A lay leader in one of America's great churches told me that he had not heard a sermon on the Holy Spirit from the renowned pulpit of his church in thirty years! A whole generation in that church could honestly repeat the Scripture, "We have never heard that there is a Holy Spirit." It is possible to preach Christ, the Cross, outline the plan of salvation, and stir people with the admonitions of Christian ethics without helping them to experience the power of the Holy Spirit.

Over the years, I have always been involved with what I call an "Apollos Adventurers" group. I'm a part of such a group here in Washington. We have all had extensive training in speech and rhetoric, pastoral leadership, and Bible teaching. Each month we come together to log in our month's activities in seeking to be book-of-Acts leaders. We usually need to be checked, corrected, convicted. More than that, we need to be loved. A meeting seldom goes by without a confession of our abject need for the Holy Spirit and His gifts for our ministries. If new life is breaking out in the churches or in my work in the Senate, it can be traced back to the quality we share together in the communion of the Holy Spirit.

It would be startling if we drove by a church today and noticed that its name had been changed from "Old First Church" to the "Church of Saint Apollos." There's no pastor who wouldn't want a church filled with people like Apollos unless he or she has never met an Aquila or Priscilla! And if you are looking for a new name to call yourself as a focus of your spiritual pilgrimage, try Apollos. Become like him, and you will become a part of the Holy Order of Those for Whom Religion Is Not Enough!

15
Courage through the Holy Spirit

Acts 19:8–20:38

We all need courage. Life has a way of dishing out more than we can take on our own. Dorothy Bernard said, "Courage is fear that has said its prayers." I'd like to put that differently: Courage is the indwelling power of the Holy Spirit released through us when we pray.

Jesus warned His disciples that they would face difficulties. He also promised that they would receive the special gift of courage. The Holy Spirit gives us courage to confront our culture, to deal with organized efforts to oppose the gospel, and to strengthen others in their battle to survive secular humanism.

A consideration of the Holy Spirit in the book of Acts needs to follow the progression of the unfolding drama portrayed. This requires a faithful study of passages where the Holy Spirit is the unmentioned source of courage during Paul's travels to Ephesus where he dealt with secularism and pagan cults, to Jerusalem where he faced traditionalism, and finally to Rome where he confronted raw military might. The travelogue from the end of chapter 20 through the completion of Acts 28 can seem arduous unless we see it as a revelation of how the Holy Spirit gives courage for life's crises.

Temples, Cults, and Superstition

When Paul arrived on the scene in Ephesus for nearly three years of ministry, he needed courage from the Holy Spirit to be faithful in this Vanity Fair of the ancient world. We should have no trouble understanding that marketplace of Asia Minor. All we need to do is look at what is going on in our own cities and we will have captured the mood and muddle of Ephesus. Superstition, sorcery, spiritualism, star worship, and sophistry pervaded the city. What a place to preach the gospel. Better yet, what a gospel to preach in such a place!

Ephesus had been built at the mouth of the Cayster River. The city became known as the "Treasure House of Asia" because it commanded the trade into the river valley of the rich province of Asia Minor. Voluptuous sensualism dominated the city. It was called an "assize town" because the Roman governor tried cases there and brought with him the pomp and pageantry of Rome. The Pan-Ionian Games were held there, affording not only recognition but revenue for the city.

The opulent Temple of Artemis was one of the seven wonders of the then-known world. One hundred and twenty-seven Parian marble pillars distinguished its exterior, some of them inlaid with gold and precious jewels. A study of its architecture reveals that it was 425 feet long, 220 feet wide, and 60 feet high. Inside was the pride of Ephesus—an altar carved by the famous Greek sculptor Praxiteles. On it was the black, multi-breasted image of Artemis, supposed to have fallen from the stars to assure fertility and prosperity.

That kind of superstition will always be capitalized on, and the silversmiths of Ephesus did just that. They made silver shrines of Artemis and sold them for a profit that brought them great wealth. The city became a cesspool, attracting every kind of magic worker and cultist in the region. In addition there were criminals of all types— murderers, swindlers, and con artists who were given asylum if they could reach the precincts of the temple. Superstition was not limited to the temple or the powers of Artemis. Charms and spells from Ephesus were sold all over the world, among them the "Ephesian

grammata," or Ephesian letters, charms that were supposed to guar-
antee safety, fertility, success, and love.

With this background we can better understand the triumphs and
the tragedies of Paul's ministry in Ephesus. He began ministering in
the synagogue, but the stubbornness and disbelief of the Jews drove
him to the Gentiles. With them his Holy Spirit-empowered preaching
of Christ had great success. Luke tells us that Paul taught in the
lecture hall of the philosopher Tyrannus daily from 11:00 A.M. until
4:00 P.M. Those were customarily hours of rest, when all work stopped
and people rested—but not the Holy Spirit. He gave Paul great
power, and news of the Christian movement spread all over the
province of Asia.

Miracles or Magic?

It wasn't long before the gospel directly confronted the culture of
Ephesus, as we read in Acts 19. Evil had a death grip on the city and
was not about to let go without a desperate battle. Then, as now,
conflict with the Lordship of Christ was fueled by superstition, spiritualism, and sophistry.

Paul's powerful message produced hundreds of new Christians, but
the extraordinary miracles he performed agitated the superstitious.
The apostle worked at a trade while in Ephesus. The handkerchiefs
and aprons he used as a workman were carried away to be placed on
the sick; his sweatband and tentmaker's apron were believed to have
the apostle's power (Acts 19:12). *New grammata*, the people thought.
And they worked. People were healed of diseases and evil spirits left
them. How gracious of God! He met the people where they were.
The name of Jesus alone had power over sickness and possession. But
we suspect that Paul did not allow the name of Jesus to be a new
form of superstition. He helped people to know the One who was
the source of the miraculous power.

Itinerant Jewish exorcists who neither knew the Savior nor had
surrendered their lives to His Lordship tried to use the name of Jesus
to exorcise people of evil spirits. Their formula was to say, "I adjure
you by the Jesus whom Paul proclaims" (19:13). The seven sons of
a priest named Sceva got an answer they had not expected. The evil

spirit they were trying to cast out responded, "Jesus I know, and Paul I know, but who are you?" Who indeed! The only one who can use the name of Jesus is one in whom the Spirit of Jesus dwells. The exorcists wanted to exploit the power they had observed in Paul without having a relationship with the Savior he preached; they were selling a religion. But Paul had not come to spiritualistic Ephesus for the purpose of adding one more mysterious spirit to the constellation of spirits that demanded no moral responsibility.

The same is true today. When people use the name of Jesus carelessly for personal gain without personal commitment to Him, they call forth not Jesus, but the forces of evil. He will not be manipulated! Yet for some people, the Christian faith represents little more than the imagined answer to their desire for magic. We want what we want when we want it, and on our terms. But Jesus is not an errand boy. He works miracles, not tricks of magic. And the greatest miracle is the transformation of a human heart by the power of love. Anything after that is a blessing we gratefully receive with thanksgiving, but can never demand.

The exorcists and magic workers of Ephesus had not listened and responded to the gospel. Because they did not know Jesus, whose name they used, they were attacked by the very spirits they wanted to exorcise for profit. Luke tells us vividly that the sons of Sceva were overpowered and beaten by the demons they tried to cast out.

Seeing what happened to Sceva's sons brought about a moral revolution in Ephesus. Those who practiced magic and sorcery brought their manuals of the black arts and burned them so that everyone could see. The implication is that they turned from magic to Christ; Luke says that "the word of the Lord grew mightily and prevailed" (19:20). That's always the result of confession, repentance, and a radical change of lifestyle.

In Ephesus, the moral reformation was far-reaching. It cut right to the heart of the silver shrine business and into the pockets of the silversmiths. The worst manifestation of evil that confronted Paul and the followers of the Way was the sophistry of the silversmiths. They mustered every fallacious argument to expose Paul and his followers as the cause of the diminishing trade and profits in Artemis silver icons.

A near riot ensued. The silversmiths chanted, "Great is Artemis of the Ephesians!" What they really were saying was, "Our livelihood is being threatened by the Way! Get rid of these Christians at all costs!" Many of the Way barely escaped with their lives. But the Lord intervened. Little did the town clerk who brought order know that he was being used to speak for the Savior of the world.

We are left to ponder the implications of the sophistry of these Ephesians for our cities. Christian history is filled with bloody memories of what happens when the gospel confronts vested interests, political pride, or economic investments. Now some of the silversmiths are in the Church! How often we practice the clever art of sophistry when we resist change, the impact of the gospel on prejudice, or Christ's judgments of social practices which cripple people. It's a demanding and dangerous business to spell out the love of Christ in practical ways. One man told me that he made two resolutions in response to the call to allow the Holy Spirit to guide his life and his business. Resolution one: to obey Christ at all costs. Resolution two: to do it even if no one else does. Only that kind of action will liberate us from equivocating sophistry.

Paul's Final Message

The fires of conflict in Ephesus forged a great church. In Acts 20, Paul pressed on to visit the churches in Macedonia and Greece, but he could not forget the Ephesian followers of the Way. They were on his mind and heart throughout the rest of the third missionary journey. On his way back to Jerusalem for a final confrontation with the Hebrew authorities, his ship made a stop at Miletus, about thirty miles from Ephesus. He sent for the elders of the Church so he could express a final word of encouragement and affirmation.

The meeting of Paul with the elders was an occasion of mixed joy and sadness. The Ephesians were delighted to see their beloved friend again, but they knew that his courageous determination to go to Jerusalem would surely mean persecution and trial, perhaps death. Paul wanted these new Christians to lead a movement. To do so, they had to keep on growing and to stay constantly open to the Holy Spirit's power over all the forces of evil in their city. What

they needed to lead the Church was also the most profound need in
their own lives. The greater the difficulties they would face, the
more courage would be given them. The Church would never be
out of danger.

Paul's message to the elders was filled with love and affection. He
gave them an admonition and an assurance. "Keep watch over yourselves and all the flock, of which the Holy Spirit has made you over-
seers, to shepherd the church of God that he obtained with the blood
of his own Son" (20:28). A warning followed for the unique problems
of Ephesus. "I know," he said, "that after I have gone, savage wolves
will come in among you, not sparing the flock. Some even from your
own group will come distorting the truth in order to entice the disciples to follow them" (20:29-30). The perverse forces that had resisted
Paul's ministry would persist against the Church and from within it.
The new Christians had to be fed spiritually, built up in the faith
and kept close to Christ and the fellowship if they were to survive
the threatening superstitions, pagan cults, and materialism of Ephesus.

Our Holy Inheritance

The tedious situation in that snake pit of dangerous influences is no
different in your Ephesus and mine today. The struggle to be authentic disciples is no less demanding. The more spiritually powerful we
become, the more we will be the target of satanic attack. The forces
of evil are not concerned with bland, culturally captured churches.

In our culture, as in Ephesus, the external influences must be coun-
teracted with internal power from the Holy Spirit. Paul's final word
to the elders is an assurance of the resources for the battle: "And now
I commend you to God and to the message of his grace, a message
that is able to build you up and to give you the inheritance among
all who are sanctified" (20:32). The source of power and the results
belong to God. He will finish what He has begun.

The apostle wanted the Ephesians to claim the implications of that
inheritance of sanctification, and we have the same need today. It is
the only antidote for satanic influence. What is holy belongs to God
and bears His nature. The inheritance of sanctification means that we
are joint heirs with Christ, and we are to become like Jesus. The

Holy Spirit is instigator and enabler of the process. In our sanctification, we grow in the image of Christ in our thoughts, feelings, words, and actions—but as a gift, not as an achievement of our efforts. We can love with His love and are able to forgive by His grace. We are energized by His power and are released to face the future with His hope. We won't make it in our own Ephesus without that. But, take courage! The Lord will never let go of you.

16
The Resiliency of the Holy Spirit

Acts 21–26

The Holy Spirit makes us resilient. He works within us to prevent us from becoming defeated by life's strains and depleted by its stresses. We never give up because of His presence and power in us. He produces indomitable resilience, which helps us become "Easter people." Then we can live courageously with the knowledge that Christ's Resurrection has defeated death, frustration, and despair.

Christ's death on the Cross assures us that we are forgiven and can live a life of freedom and joy, but it is the Resurrection that gives us the power to live that new life through daily pressures. The celebration of Christ's victory is alive in every moment, relationship, situation, or problem. The realization of Christ's Resurrection enables our own; we will be alive forever and therefore are truly alive right now. We have died to our own control of our lives and have been resurrected to a new dimension of living in Christ; we have become the post-Resurrection dwelling of the living Lord. We will never be alone again, for He is with us and in us. We can face anything because the same power that raised Jesus from the dead is at work in us.

Acts 21–26 gives us Luke's dramatic account of Paul's arrest, imprisonment, and repeated trials in Jerusalem and Caesarea on the way to Rome. I have found it helpful to deal with these chapters as a whole. The central theme is the Resurrection: the *hope* of the Resurrection brought Paul back to Jerusalem; the *truth* of the Resurrection was the conclusive thrust of his witness in each trial; the *power* of the Resurrection was his source of strength in prison.

Through the events of Luke's account I want to show how the power of the Resurrection we see in Paul's faith can be ours. I believe that the same uncrushable resiliency that springs back after his difficulties is available to us today—because Christ lives.

Paul's Radiant Hope

"God worked extraordinary miracles through Paul" (Acts 19:11) as he journeyed throughout Asia, preaching the gospel and encouraging new believers. Now, in Acts 21, we find him striding courageously into the city of Jerusalem and into the clutches of his enemies. The Resurrection was his only reason for going, his only hope of power to withstand what he knew would happen there, his only message to proclaim.

There is no other way to explain the brave apostle's audacity. Paul lived in two realms: the visible, transitory world of change, hatred, corruption, negativism, and death and the invisible realm of the Resurrection in fellowship with a risen Savior who had defeated death, sin, the powers of darkness, and discouragement. That's why he could write the Roman Christians: "May the God of hope fill you with all joy and peace in your faith, that by the *power of the Holy Spirit,* your whole life and outlook may be radiant with hope" (Rom. 15:13, PHILLIPS, italics added).

Paul's radiant hope was centered on the Resurrection. It was the heart of the gospel for him. A few months before entering Jerusalem, while at Ephesus, he had written to the Corinthians that without the Resurrection there would be no hope.

If there is no resurrection of the dead, then Christ has not been raised; and if Christ has not been raised, then our proclamation has been in vain and your faith has been in vain. . . . If Christ has

not been raised, your faith is futile and you are still in your sins. . . .
If for this life only we have hoped in Christ, we are of all people
most to be pitied. (1 Cor. 15:13-19)

The Cross without the Resurrection is just another tragic death of a
good man; faith is empty; the Christian life is a pitiful, self-generated
wish-dream. But crowned by the Resurrection, and enabled by the
resurrected Lord, the daily life of a Christian is liberated by the Cross
and has abundant assurance, now and forever.

That fact alone enables us to understand Paul's emotional stability,
mental outlook, and incredible confidence when his faith was under
fire in trial and imprisonment. Anyone with a lesser hope would
have been despondent and despairing. Not Paul. He had known persistent sickness, rejection by his people, resistance from fellow Christians, and constant physical persecution. Something he wrote just
before the trial in Jerusalem gives us the key to understand how the
Resurrection and the present, powerful Savior kept him from giving up:

We are pressed on every side by trouble, but not crushed and
broken. We are perplexed because we don't know why things happen as they do, but we don't give up and quit. We are hunted
down, but God never abandons us. We get knocked down, but
we get up again and keep going. These bodies of ours are constantly
facing death just as Jesus did; so it is clear to all that it is only the
living Christ within [who keeps us safe] (2 Cor. 4:8-10, TLB).

The Resilient Power of the Resurrection

The first aspect of Resurrection resiliency appeared when Paul arrived
in Jerusalem and went to the leaders of the Church. His report of
what had been happening in his ministry was filled with joy—amazing, after all he'd been through. With excitement he told James and
the Church fathers what the uplifted, ubiquitous Lord had done
among the Gentiles. They rejoiced with Paul, but he also presented
them with a problem. Conflict was raging over his ministry, and
rumors were flying everywhere that he was telling Jews among the
Gentiles to forsake the law of Moses.

The particular concern of the Church was for the converted Jews who had swelled the ranks of Christians in Jerusalem. Something had to be done to clarify the apostle's position. What they recommended may have helped the Jewish Christian, but it brought Paul into direct conflict with the established Sanhedrin. Note how the living Christ freed Paul up to participate in a compromise for unity. After all he'd been through, it must have seemed silly, if not stupid. But the truth of the Resurrection had made Paul responsive and resilient.

Following instructions from the Church leaders, Paul gave money to four Jewish Christians who were taking the Nazarite vow in the temple (21:23-24). An expression of gratitude to God, the vow involved abstention from eating meat, drinking wine, and cutting of hair. The final seven days were to be spent in the temple courts. At the conclusion of the time, offerings would be made of a year-old lamb as a sin offering, a ram as a peace offering, a meat-and-drink offering, and a basket of unleavened bread and cakes. (No wonder a sponsor was needed to pay for their time away from work and for the expensive offerings.) Finally, the supplicant's hair was to be shaved as an outward sign of the inner oblation. Paul's participation was meant by the Church to be a final and vivid affirmation of the law of Moses for both the confused Hebrew Christians in the Church and the priests in the temple.

Paul's resilience seemed to have no limits as he cooperated wholeheartedly in the efforts at reconciliation. The Resurrection does that to a person. We are free to be flexible and adjustable as a part of the fellowship. That kind of maturity comes from ultimate trust in the present Savior. Paul did not demand to do things his way. Liberated by a great vision, he was on his way to Rome for the risen Master! His winsome willingness to do anything that would strengthen the ministry of the Church in Jerusalem was a direct result. What the Sanhedrin did to distort his obedience to the fellowship would not in any way diminish the evidence of Resurrection freedom in his witness.

Lies and Accusations
But the Church's reconciliation strategy backfired. It was Pentecost

time and Jerusalem was filled with Jews. Some had come from the Roman province of Asia that Paul had just left. They were more than pilgrims to the Holy City; they were determined to destroy the apostle Paul, once and for all.

They had seen him in the temple but had also watched him in Jerusalem with a Gentile convert from Asia named Trophimus. They put the two things together to make an untrue and inflammatory accusation: they charged Paul with taking Trophimus into the sacred precincts of the temple. They were sure they had the ancient Law on their side. An inscription on the wall of the temple stated: "No man of alien race is to enter within the balustrade and fence that goes around the temple, and if anyone is taken in the act, let him know that he has himself to blame for the penalty of death that follows." The charge was a lie, of course, but the Jews knew that the Romans allowed the death sentence for the offense.

The Asian Jews incited a riot, supported by the leaders of Israel, crying out, "Fellow Israelites, help! This is the man who is teaching everyone everywhere against our people, our law, and this place; more than that, he has actually brought Greeks into the temple and has defiled this holy place" (21:28). Taking "justice" into their own hands, they seized Paul, dragged him out of the temple, and proceeded to try to kill him by beating and stoning. Jerusalem fell into confusion, which brought out the Roman tribune, Claudius Lysias, with centurions and soldiers.

Seeing that Paul was about to be beaten to death but unable to make out the charge from the angry, jeering mob, Lysias interceded and arrested him. His soldiers chained the apostle and actually had to carry his broken and bleeding body out of the mob. The tribune quickly ordered him taken to the Tower of Antonia, connected to the outer court of the temple on the northwestern side. The crowds followed with bloodthirsty cries, "Away with him!"

Infused with Physical Strength

Look at the physical resiliency of the resurrected Lord in Paul. As he was being carried away, under the immediate protection of the tribune (who had mistaken Paul for an Egyptian leader of the Assassins), Paul identified himself as a Jew, a citizen of Tarsus, and begged to speak to the people again. Lysias must have had mingled feelings of amazement and admiration at that. What grit and courage! The power of the Lord living in Paul came out not only in physical endurance and spiritual courage, but also in charismatic prowess when he was blessed to speak again. When Paul stood on the steps and began to speak in Hebrew, a great hush fell on the crowd. His body was swollen from beating and blood streamed down his face, but his full powers quickly sprang back to full force.

There is an indomitable, artesian physical resiliency in those who have realized the Resurrection. This has been true throughout Christian history. Not only does the indwelling Lord release latent, untapped energies, He miraculously infuses us with strength beyond our own. I have experienced this repeatedly. When I am too exhausted to move, the Lord provides the strength to do what He has willed. When I feel beaten by circumstances or problems and the courage to go on seems to have run out, I realize that I have used only the surface resources of human energy; beneath are the limitless powers of the Lord.

Paul knew this better than any man who has ever lived. When Lysias watched his prisoner hold the crowd in rapt attention, he wondered how Paul could do it, beaten as he was. The tribune realized that this was no ordinary man he had arrested.

Paul's defense quickly outlined his heritage as a Jew, his training as a Pharisee under Gamaliel, his zealous vigilance of the observance of the law, and his persecution of the Way. Then he boldly told the crowd of his encounter with the resurrected Messiah and his commission to bear witness to all the world. Strength grew as he spoke. But when he stated that "all the world" included Gentiles, the mob's wrath blazed up again. "Away with such a fellow from the earth! For he should not be allowed to live" (22:22). They expressed their rage according to the custom of the day: shouting, waving garments, and throwing dust into the air.

Once again Lysias had to step in to save his prisoner. This time he took no chances. To obtain a confession of what Paul had been up to in Jerusalem, he ordered Paul imprisoned and flogged. (Flogging, or scourging, was a beating with leather thongs intertwined with bone and metal.) In preparation Paul was stretched out and tied.

What well-timed sagacity Paul displayed! Believing himself destined for Rome, he had no intention of surrendering his life in this manner. Just as the thongs were lifted for the first strikes, Paul cried out words that turned the centurion extortioner's face pale with fear: "Is it legal for you to flog a Roman citizen who is uncondemned?" (Scourging a Roman citizen could mean death to the one inflicting the punishment.) The centurion dropped his whip and ran to the tribune's chambers. "What are you about to do? This man is a Roman citizen." Now Lysias and the soldier were both frightened. The tribune was further amazed at his prisoner when he questioned Paul with the respect due a Roman citizen. How could Lysias explain the resourcefulness of this man of Tarsus? He was not physically powerful, his physique was not impressive, and yet he seemed unconquerable by the emotional and physical strain he'd been through.

The Audacious Power of Truth

Lysias, determined to get to the bottom of the charge against this remarkable prisoner, arranged a hearing before the Jewish rulers of the Sanhedrin. Perhaps he hoped that would end his responsibility for this strange mixture of Jew and Roman he had in chains. But once again Paul astounded him.

Completely unafraid and unimpressed with the imposing array of rulers, Paul strode in before them and began to speak, "Brothers, up to this day I have lived my life with a clear conscience before God" (23:1). The tempers of the Sanhedrin were raw, and Paul barely got the words out before Ananias ordered him to be struck on the mouth for blasphemy. Now we see the fearlessness of his resiliency. With prophetic boldness like that of an Old Testament prophet he faced his accuser: "God will strike you, you whitewashed wall! Are you sitting to judge me according to the law, and yet in violation of the law you order me to be struck?"

Paul could not have used a more inflammatory term. *A whitewashed wall!* It was the custom to whitewash tombs containing dead bodies to alert an Israelite of the danger of ceremonial defilement

incurred by touching the dead. Ananias deserved the defamatory ap-
pellation. He was a glutton, an unjust ruler, and a capricious quisling
in league with Rome. Yet, Paul had overstepped. He knew the law
forbade speaking evil of the high priest, but Paul was unaware of
Ananias's new position (23:5). Paul quickly acknowledged his indis-
cretion, but he did not retract his accusation. The record stood.

Then Paul pressed on to his real purpose and passion. He knew
that the Sanhedrin was made up of Sadducees, who did not believe
in resurrection or a life beyond death, and of Pharisees, who did. He
wanted them to know exactly where he stood. The unmistakable
certainty in the apostle's faith not only of resurrection, but Christ's
Resurrection, is stated pointedly. Here before the Sanhedrin, the highest court of his people, he wanted to expose the vibrant pulsebeat of
Christianity: "I am on trial concerning the hope of the resurrection
of the dead" (23:6). Paul proclaimed two inseparable realities: (1) Jesus
the Christ was the fulfillment of the messianic hope; (2) Jesus had
been raised from the dead and was alive. Paul's own experience of
this tandem truth gave him assurance that because Christ was alive,
he too was a recipient of eternal life that death could not end. He
could take anything with that hope.

The Sanhedrin was thrown into new conflict over an old dispute.
The Sadducees and Pharisees lined up on different sides of the issue.
The dissension between the rulers took the heat off Paul, though
once again violence ensued and the tribune had to step in to protect
the imprisoned Roman citizen. But Paul accomplished the purpose
for which he had come to Jerusalem: to witness to the power of
Christ's Resurrection.

Assurance from the Master

Back in the barracks the following night, Paul received encouragement. He had held the line on his belief that Jesus was alive and now
the same Jesus came to him to give assurance. Paul's unswerving witness to the truth was rewarded with an undeniable experience of the
reality. Luke tells us that "the Lord stood by him." What more did
Paul need than that? What greater help can any of us have than that
when our faith is under fire?

What the Lord said to Paul He says to us: "Keep up your courage! For just as you have testified for me in Jerusalem, so you must bear witness also in Rome" (23:11). The words were drenched in dynamic strength. "Stay strong, Paul. This is neither the worst nor the last of it. I am with you; We're going to Rome together. Keep your attention on that. We are going to penetrate the center of political power in Rome to change the world. I am in charge; trust Me!" With that assurance, Paul could face anything knowing he was not alone. After that Paul was all the more determined.

But so were the forty Jews who had banded together to keep pressure on the rulers who had briefly lost their determination in internal conflict. Hatred has its twisted vows, and they made one now, swearing not to eat or drink until Paul was dead. A hunger strike is a powerful pressure ploy. This one brought the Sanhedrin back into line as they devised a clever scheme to get Paul back before them so that vigilantes could ambush and kill him as he was being brought from the prison.

But the Lord's people were also at work in Jerusalem. When word of the intrigue reached the Church, Paul's nephew was dispatched to warn him. He in turn sent the young man directly to the tribune. This settled it for Lysias. Paul was too hot to handle in Jerusalem. There was nothing to do but send him to Caesarea to be judged by Felix, the Roman governor. We are amazed by the precautions the tribune took to protect his prisoner, assigning 200 soldiers, 70 horsemen, and 200 spearmen as guards for the journey. In reality, there were 471 people watching over this one Roman Jew: 470 soldiers, spearmen, horsemen, *and* the Savior of the world. The Lord was keeping watch over His own. No wonder Paul's faith was resilient!

Paul On Trial

The account in Acts 24–26 of Paul's repeated arraignments and trials in Caesarea is a study in lugubrious Roman jurisprudence and human befuddlement. First one governor and then another tried to handle the case, while still seeking to maintain Roman law and keep peace with the rebellious Jews. None succeeded.

Felix, the first to try, was a complex, ambitious man with a distorted record. It was through the influence of his brother Pallos, a favorite of Nero, that Felix had risen from being a slave to a powerful governor. He never lived down his humble origins, however. The Roman historian Tacitus said of him, "He exercised the prerogatives of a king with the spirit of a slave." His lust for power had moved him through three propitious marriages, the last to Drusilla, the daughter of Herod Agrippa I. His record of intrigue and greed places him in sharp contrast to the brilliant Pharisee of Tarsus he was destined to try to judge. Little did the unscrupulous Felix know that he, not Paul, was on trial—and before eternal court.

It took only five days for Ananias and the Jews to track Paul to Caesarea. They brought with them Tertullus, one of the most eloquent and clever trial lawyers of Jerusalem, to present their case before Felix. But neither Tertullus's flattery of Felix nor his flagrant demeaning of Paul was a match for the apostle's brilliant witness. Paul stated his case flatly: "With respect to the resurrection of the dead I am on trial before you this day" (24:21). He held the line, however great the forces opposing him in the verbal tug-of-war.

Paul won the day: the governor returned him to custody and showed his partiality by allowing Paul's friends the privilege of visiting him. Felix was obviously moved and bargained for more time. He was knowledgeable about Christianity and apparently well aware that he should be cautious in any quick decision. More than that, he wanted to learn more about this strange hope in the Resurrection Paul talked about. Along with his wife Drusilla, Felix listened to Paul privately on several occasions, although his capacity to hear the clear message about Christ was muddled by the dubious quality of his own moral life and his mixed emotions. His interest was piqued by the power of Christ, but punctured by incisive justice, self-control, and the future judgment Paul proclaimed.

Felix missed a God-given opportunity to experience the abundant life and live forever because he did not want his past disturbed nor his motives purified. Two years later his attempts at clever intrigue got him into trouble with Rome over the way he handled a conflict between Jews and Greeks in Caesarea. He was deposed and transferred, leaving his post without either political or spiritual power.

Festus, a different breed of governor, replaced Felix. He had hardly set foot on his new territory as governor when he was besieged by the leaders of the Jews. Over two years had passed and still their anger burned white-hot. Eight days in Jerusalem convinced the new governor that he had better try the case in the relative safety and sanity of Caesarea, but the trial brought no more resolution than before.

The same absurd charges came from the Jews and the same assured courage was seen in Paul. In one momentous difference this time, however, Paul's declaration of innocence ended with an appeal to be tried by Caesar. Every Roman citizen had that right, and Paul was under orders from his Master to go to Rome. Festus seemed relieved. He would get out of the responsibility to judge the nasty mess much more easily than he thought. "You have appealed to the emperor; to the emperor you shall go," Festus replied (25:12).

Holy Spirit Eloquence

One further scene remained in the dramatic act exposing Paul's resiliency in Caesarea. Jesus had once told his followers:

> Beware of them, for they will hand you over to councils and flog you in their synagogues; and you will be dragged before governors and kings because of me, as a testimony to them and the Gentiles. When they hand you over, do not worry about how you are to speak or what you are to say; for what you are to say will be given to you at that time; for it is not you who speak, but the Spirit of your Father speaking through you. (Matt. 10:17-20)

Paul had known all things that the Lord predicted and promised, except one. Now, King Herod Agrippa II was to fulfill that prophecy, and the Lord's promise of Holy Spirit-inspired eloquence would never be more evident. Agrippa II and his wife Bernice arrived in Caesarea to welcome Festus. What happened to Agrippa there would nearly persuade him to become a Christian.

The End of the Herods

All of the King Herods were strangely entangled with Christ. Herod

Agrippa II was the last of the Herods to meddle with Christ or His followers. His great-grandfather was the King Herod who had feared the birth of the Christ child and murdered the male children in the vicinity of Bethlehem. The grand-uncle of Agrippa II had murdered John the Baptist; and his father, Agrippa I, had executed James, imprisoned Peter, and had been eaten by worms as a punishment for allowing people to worship him as a god right there in Caesarea (Acts 12:20-23). Bernice was a sister of Drusilla, Felix's wife, and therefore actually sister of Agrippa II. What a sick, infested family tree!

After Festus briefed the king on general affairs, he brought his attention to the strange case before him concerning Paul of Tarsus. He knew that Agrippa had personal knowledge of the Jewish religion and supposed he might help him in dealing with the complexities of the troublesome Pharisee. The problem was clear: the Sanhedrin would not relent and Paul would not recant. To complicate matters, Festus told the king, Paul had appealed to Caesar. Like his family before him, Herod could not resist the impulse to get involved in something to do with Christ or His followers.

The sheer drama of Paul's appearance before Agrippa and Bernice grips our imagination. The king and his sister were arrayed in the splendid purple robes of royalty. Festus, in honor of the king, was probably wearing his scarlet governor's robe. The court was decorated for the occasion and guarded by captains, centurions, and legionnaires. Now picture the apostle as he is brought before these imposing earthly powers. He is stooped, small in stature, and physically unimposing. The chains dangle about his gnarled hands. But the expression on his face is magnetic and his eyes glint in majesty. When he speaks, his voice cuts through the pretentious elegance of the Hall of Audience built by Herod the Great. Paul was neither impressed by Agrippa nor afraid of the Roman power.

Proclaiming the Resurrection

Agrippa gave his permission to speak, and Paul rose to the occasion with soaring rhetoric. He retold his story and once again proclaimed the power of the Resurrection. "It is for this hope, your Excellency, I am accused by Jews! Why is it thought incredible by any of you that God raises the dead?" (26:7-8). His heavenly vision was not denied as he recounted his encounter with Jesus on the road to Damascus, concluding:

> To this day I have had help from God, and so I stand here, testifying to both small and great, saying nothing but what the prophets and Moses said would take place: that the Messiah must suffer, and that, by being the first to rise from the dead, he would proclaim light both to our people and to the Gentiles. (26:22-23)

It was obvious that Agrippa was moved and disturbed by the gospel. The resurrected Lord drove Paul's words like arrows into the king's heart. He felt convicted and unsettled. Festus realized how rattled the king had become with the situation. "Paul," Festus said, "your great learning is turning you mad!"

Paul, unimpressed with Festus' ridicule, did not take his eyes off Agrippa. Holding intense eye-to-eye contact with the king, he responded to Festus.

> I am not out of my mind, most excellent Festus, but I am speaking the sober truth. Indeed the king knows about these things, and *to him* I speak freely; for I am certain that none of these things has escaped his notice, for this was not done in a corner. (26:25-26, emphasis mine)

Note how Paul moved in on Herod: "King Agrippa, do you believe in the prophets? I know that you believe." Agrippa knew where Paul was leading. If he believed in the prophets, he would believe in the Messiah, and that would demand a decision about Jesus and the Resurrection. But what could he say before that auspicious gathering in the magnificence of his grandfather's Great Hall? Paul was leading him up to an encounter with the Lord and he knew it. The gift of faith leapt within him, but then he remembered who and where he was. He had to uphold the dignity of his depleted family name. Enough of this! "In a short time you think to make me a Christian?"

Paul's response was the result of the Resurrection power in him, the undeniable desire for all to find what he has found: "I pray to God that not only you but also all who are listening to me today might become such as I am—except for these chains" (26:29).

That's the power of personal witness, the dynamic of relational evangelism. Unless we can say that we want everyone to know what we know, we have missed the excitement of the Christian life. Can we say, like Paul, that we want people to become what we are? Many of us would shrink from that, unsatisfied by what we have allowed Christ to do in us. We would not want others to have the same incomplete, unsatisfying, inadequate experience of Christ we have. Do we want a duplication not just of our convictions, but of our character? Paul wanted both for Agrippa. If we do not want to multiply what we are, there is something wrong.

Nothing Is Impossible

Though Festus and Agrippa did not have the courage to respond to Paul's challenge, the impact of the gospel came upon them. They mustered enough courage to resist pressure from the Sanhedrin, saying to one another, "This man is doing nothing to deserve death or imprisonment." Agrippa even went so far as to say, "This man could have been set free if he had not appealed to the emperor" (26:31-32). Roman law required that once the appeal had been made by a Roman citizen, it must be carried out. Paul must go to Rome. But only Paul knew the real reason—not Roman law or even his appeal: *Christ* had destined him to go to Rome, and neither the angry Jews nor all the legions of the emperor could keep him from his heavenly vision.

Something has happened to me as I have lived in the apostle's skin through his two years in prison and on trial. It has reminded me of the ebullient power of the Resurrection. Christ is alive! Jesus' words echo in my heart: "Because I live you shall live also." His Resurrection makes possible my own. Nothing is impossible now. The crushed hopes and dreams, the depleted energy and vision, the collapsed determination and daring all spring back to life. I have rediscovered the power of the Resurrection for living every hour.

My deepest prayer is that you will too. The Holy Spirit is ready to give you resiliency through an hourly realization of Resurrection power.

> For resurrection living there's resurrection power,
> And oh, the joy of living in each hour!
> For all of life's an Eastertide
> For those who in the Spirit abide.

17
Living the New Chapter of the Book of Acts

Acts 28

When I did graduate studies in Scotland, I had the thrilling experience of sailing on the *Queen Mary* from New York to Southampton. She was a magnificent ship. Though my student's budget allowed only double "D" deck, I used to spend most of my time up on the top deck walking, with the cold salt winds blowing in my face.

I can remember admiring the gallant determination with which the historic craft cut through the high waves. With typical British efficiency the organized crew kept everything working in perfect order. As I strolled on deck, I would try to recapture the feeling of what it must have been like aboard the "Mary" as a lovely pleasure vessel and then as a troop ship carefully evading the German submarines during World War II.

The next time I saw the *Queen Mary* she had become a museum piece. Her last voyage ended in Long Beach harbor, where her gigantic engine had been removed. She sat there motionless, attached tightly to the dock. Souvenir shops lined her decks. The refurbished cabins had been transformed into hotel rooms. Actors with studied British accents played the parts of the crew. I thought: *The one thing the Queen Mary will never be able to do again is to fulfill the reason for which she was built—to sail the high seas.*

Like this great ship, you and I and our churches were meant for the adventure of the high seas. Our congregations mustn't become museum pieces of past glory, but restored ships to sail in the turbulent waters of our own time. We are not meant to be actors who pretend but crew members who sail with a mission. We must put our engines back into the ship, clear our decks of impedimenta, and start sailing again.

The book of Acts can be the chartbook and sailing instructions for getting your Queen Mary and mine back to sea. The challenge of preparing for the Holy Spirit's power in the first chapter of Acts charts our course. The final chapter of Acts serves as both compass and sextant for us as we move on in our lives in the Spirit. And we must continue the story, filling our own new chapters with the wonders of God's power for everyday living.

The quality of contagious new life in the first century described by Luke—the Spirit's power, the energetic Church on the move—is available to every generation. Acts leaves us with the impression, "It's up to you now to continue. What you have learned about the early Church will be a challenge for the Church always." We must dare to measure the Church in every age by the vision and vitality of the first Church, which was empowered by the acts of the Holy Spirit.

Paul Welcomed to Rome

Following a perilous sea voyage and shipwreck on Malta, Paul finally arrived at the Italian port of Puteoli (Acts 28:11-13). Under the guard of Julius and the Roman legionnaires, he and his friends traveled along the Appian Way, which led from the coast to Rome. The Christians in Rome had received word of Paul's arrival and could not wait to see him. They sent a deputation to welcome him with joy. The Greek word used here is the same as for a welcoming party sent out to meet a conquering general or king. The jubilant greeters met the honored apostle at the Forum of Appius and the Three Taverns, stops along the Appian Way. The underground communications network of Christians had kept them informed about everything that Paul had been through.

Life had not been easy for the Church at Rome either. Some historians suggest that the fellowship had grown from a small nucleus of Jews who had been in Jerusalem at that historic Pentecost when the first Church was born. The infant Church in Rome expanded despite difficulties as Hebrew-Christian travelers and merchants settled there. Many Jews were of the Liberti—those who had been slaves and had purchased their freedom. Added to Jewish converts were Roman believers who were secret followers of the Lord. Christianity had become a vital movement, and there was a strong Church anxiously awaiting the apostle.

The long-awaited visit of the famous leader finally became a reality. Pent-up joy exploded when the Roman Christians embraced and greeted their hero of hope. Love and affection drenched the parched, weary spirit of the exhausted traveler. We can only imagine the excited conversation and fellowship among Christ's people as they walked the final miles to Rome.

In the imperial city, Paul was treated with respect by Roman authorities while he waited for trial. He was given quarters under the rotating surveillance of soldiers from the praetorian guard, the private troops of the emperor. Luke tells us that Paul lived for over two years here, and was allowed to have visitors. His quarters became the center of fellowship and study among the Christians of Rome.

Dull Hearts and Closed Ears

The first thing Paul did in Rome was consistent with his usual practice in over thirty years of apostleship—he visited the synagogue. He never lost the urgency to communicate Christ to his fellow Jews, and he was never put off by their resistant responses. That's why he began his ministry in Rome by calling first for the leaders of the seven synagogues in the Trastever, the Hebrew colony. He was not free to go to the synagogues as had been his habit in every other city. No word had arrived from Jerusalem about him, and they had heard nothing bad about him. But the Jewish leaders had nothing good to say about the "sect" of which he was a leader. They were suspicious of Paul because of their encounters with Christians in Rome. They were willing to listen, but with reservations. They came to Paul's quarters with less than open minds.

Paul expounded the truth of Jesus as Messiah and the reality of the kingdom of God from morning until night, but only a few responded. Luke speaks succinctly of their bland, unimpressionable religiosity: they disbelieved, disagreed, and departed. But before they left, Paul managed to have the last word. He used Isaiah and Psalm 67 to give his diagnosis of and prognosis for spirituality gone stale. His quotation of the Lord in verses 26-27 was pointed:

> Go to this people and say,
> "You will indeed listen, but never understand,
> and you will indeed look, but never perceive.
> For this people's heart has grown dull,
> and their ears are hard of hearing,
> and they have shut their eyes;
> so that they might not look with their eyes,
> and listen with their ears,
> and understand with their heart and turn—
> and I would heal them."

What a dreary picture of religious people who have missed the point. They came to Paul's quarters for the sake of religious activity; they heard words but did not understand; they saw truth but refused to perceive. Their emotions were dull and their ears weary from the repetition of great things. The disturbing result: they could no longer see truth, discern its implications, or order their lives around it. They no longer needed or wanted God.

As I picture that group of self-righteous, judgmental people crowded into Paul's quarters in Rome, I see much of the Church in America today. Sometimes, the legacy of religion is spiritual lethargy.

What the rules and regulations, prejudice, and preconceptions did for those Jews then happens to church people today: we get bored. Our ears close up, our eyes shut, and our hearts become cold. We do not lose our faith; we merely stop shaping our lives around it.

The Dynamics of a Great Church

Now look at Luke's description of the Church in Rome. The quarters were the same, Paul was the same, and the climate in Rome was the same. But something had happened that made all the difference. When the new Christians and their inquiring friends crowded into that room, it became radiant with joy and vitality. In a final sentence Luke portrayed the true Church: "And he [Paul] lived there two whole years at his own expense, and welcomed all who came to him, proclaiming the kingdom of God and teaching about the Lord Jesus Christ with all boldness and without hindrance" (vss. 30-31).

Catch the dynamics of a great church in that statement. This was a Church focused on Christ, the kingdom of God, and an inclusive fellowship. *The Living Bible* translation catches the viable joy: "Paul lived for the next two years in his rented house and welcomed all who visited him, telling them with all boldness about the Kingdom of God and about the Lord Jesus Christ; and no one tried to stop him." Let's move backward from finish to start of this great sentence and spell out the meaning for us today.

1. The Lord Jesus Christ is the focus and force of a great church.
We exist to know Him and make Him known. When Luke tells us that Paul taught about the Lord quite openly and unhindered, that not only clarifies for me the conditions in which he taught but the quality of the content he taught. Because he was unhindered, he was uninhibited. The ambience of freedom enabled sharing of what Christ meant to the apostle and what He could also mean to the listeners. The King James Version states he taught "with all confidence." The truth of the person of Christ resonated through the life of the liberated Pharisee.

A woman I know whose husband claims he is a "recovering alcoholic" says that she is a "recovering Pharisee." Christ is at work setting her free. Her witness is not made up of what has happened, but of what is *happening.* I believe Paul was like that. His teaching was the penetrating pulsebeat of the Church because it was fresh with recent and present experiences.

That's always the key to a great church. Relational preaching and teaching is revelational truth exposed in our relationships. Christ is not a theological formulation or just a historical figure; He is a living Person. When a church not only talks about what Christ did, but what He's doing in people's lives, a dynamic power is released. Our life "in Christ" as recipients of the salvation of His death and Resurrection must be coupled with His life *in* us as the motivating, engendering Holy Spirit.

The finest compliment I ever heard given to a clergyman was, "He talks about Christ as if he knew Him." When Christ is taught and preached that way, and the life of a church becomes a fellowship in the presence of the Lord, the world will be startled and attracted. Christ alone can satisfy human hunger. He alone can sustain during times of pressure. He alone can liberate people to love. He alone can enable us to face death and be assured of eternal life.

A church focused on Christ is a personal church. Christ frees us to become more personal. By that I mean we are released from privatism to talk about what Christ means to us in the personal struggle for identity, security, affirmation, purpose, and self-worth. When we talk about Christ theoretically, we zoom over the heads and hearts of most people. When pastor, officers, and members are open to talk about what a difference Christ has made in their inner attitudes and outer feelings, others will listen and want to become part of their fellowship.

Many people have gone to church for years with broken relationships, hidden guilt, unconfessed fear, and anguished hurt lurking beneath the surface of their "church faces." They get the feeling that they alone face those problems. If the pastor in the pulpit and the people in the pews could be honest, they would find they are all alike in the human struggle. A vital church presents Christ as the vanquisher of death, but also as the liberator from all the things that keep us from living fully.

2. A truly great church lives under the mandate of the kingdom of God.
Paul proclaimed "the kingdom of God . . . with all boldness." Preaching Christ is the call to new life. Preaching the kingdom is sounding the marching orders to spread God's plan and purpose into every facet of our existence. Jesus taught that the kingdom is within, between us, in the midst, and coming in all of life. The little Church in Paul's room really believed that it had been called to be part of God's strategy of restoring His damaged and perverted creation to its original destiny. Audaciously they sought the will of the Lord for their total lives.

Elton Trueblood observed, "We are told to pray for the kingdom, which is defined as that situation in which God's will is made manifest on earth." The question we need to ask is: "Lord, what do you want us to do to realize your reign in our church and the society around us?" A church grows in power as it orders its life and ministry around the mandate of the Master.

That's when an exciting church comes alive. It is electrified by seeking the situational guidance of our Lord and then reporting back to the fellowship what is happening. The reign of Christ is sought for our relationships, our families, our places of work, our community, and our nation. The world and its problems become our parish. We need not apologize to anyone. We have the secret of abundant life: Christ is the answer to the world's complexities. Two thousand years have slipped by without much change in the world not because the gospel is impotent, but because the people of God have been too impervious to the power of the Holy Spirit and unwilling to follow His guidance.

There is an adventuresome excitement that pervades a church on the move. When people share Christ with others and work for His justice in the structures of society and support each other's vision, a fellowship is galvanized. Some of the most memorable moments of my Christian experience have occurred in small groups where people talked about areas of their lives surrendered to our Lord and what He had done with the raw material of their willingness.

In the churches where I have served as pastor and now in the United States Senate, I have witnessed the impact of small groups meeting for Bible study and for sharing of needs and prayer. These "churches in miniature" give people an opportunity to talk over the implications of the Scriptures for daily living and to become accountable to each other for how they live out their faith. Deep friendships are enabled by the Holy Spirit. People learn to encourage and care for each other.

I have been a part of a small group in each phase of my life since becoming a Christian in my freshman year of college. My conversion took place in a small group in my college dormitory. All through my education, the Holy Spirit arranged for people to join me in what I like to call spiritual adventure groups. Some of the most profound friendships of my life were formed in these groups. Our mutual accountability to the Holy Spirit and to each other kept me on track. Through the years, these groups have heightened the joy of my life in the Spirit and helped me discover the resources of the Spirit in times of difficulty and discouragement.

A senator in a group to which I belong has a way of asking me, "Well, how are you—really?" The group listens intently to my response. These people rejoice over victories, but also are there for me in challenging, tougher times. A small group is crucial for growth in trusting the Holy Spirit.

3. A dynamic church is an inclusive fellowship.

What an unlikely mixture of people gathered with Paul during his two years in Rome. There were the saints who had been faithful to Christ through the years. They had kept the Church together with little support or help against the difficulties and dangers in Rome.

Add to these Paul and his friends. We are told in the letters Paul wrote during his imprisonment that he was surrounded by his friends. Mark was there, indicating it was a fellowship of forgiveness. Mark's defection at Perga years before had been forgiven, and Paul had called for him to be at his side. We can imagine the hours of conversation, confession, and reconciliation that took place between those two.

It was also a fellowship of encouragement, for Timothy was there. He meant a great deal to Paul. As his "child in the faith" (1 Tim. 1:2), his "brother" in the Lord (1 Thess. 3:2), and his "co-worker"

(Rom. 16:21), Timothy gave a special gift of encouragement to the apostle.

It was Luke who cared for Paul's needs. There is a winsome quality to the words "Only Luke is with me" (2 Tim. 4:11). Luke had never failed Paul. The brilliant physician could provide intellectual stimulus. I believe Luke was writing Acts during these years at Rome. Can you imagine the delight they had together as they reminisced over what the Holy Spirit had done throughout their journeys? I believe Luke pressed Paul to crystallize and synthesize the implications of what they had seen and heard. And there were others: Aristarchus, Tychicus, Epaphroditus, and many others—a supportive, affirming fellowship.

No picture of the early Church in Rome is complete without looking at the Roman guards. If you read between the lines of Philippians and check historical accounts, you will find that the very sentinels who were assigned the duty of guarding Paul were magnetically drawn into the inclusive fellowship. Paul said he was thankful for his imprisonment because it advanced the gospel; he went on to tell the Philippians, "it has become known throughout the whole imperial guard and to everyone else that my imprisonment is for Christ" (Phil. 1:13). There are historians who suggest that the guards had to be changed repeatedly because of the rapid rate of their conversion. The reason that news spread through the praetorian guard so quickly was that converted guards could not resist telling what had happened to them.

Picture a guard watching this fellowship in action; feel the warm, accepting fellowship soften and penetrate his heart. A guard could not last very long in Paul's quarters without meeting the Lord and seeing his own life in the light of the kingdom. There was a contagious quality of life, which few guards could resist. The cross-cultural, interracial fellowship was made up of all ages, both sexes, different backgrounds, and a multiplicity of personality types. That's always a sign of a great church.

4. A mark of a vital church is that it exists for those beyond it.
Luke tells us that Paul "welcomed all who came to him." *The Living*

Bible says that "all who visited were welcomed." Word spread throughout Rome that something was happening! All inquirers were included with acceptance and affirmation. The quality of life not only attracted them, but showed them how they too could live. Evangelism is not only going out to others; it's modeling life as it was meant to be for people the Lord has brought in to observe.

Every contemporary church must ask, "If an outsider, an onlooker, were to observe the life of our church, would he or she want to find our Lord and become one with us in the adventure?" Any church that is truly living the new chapter of Acts in our time is living so close to Christ that its doors are open. Outsiders should be able to see saints there whose lives are so radiant with joy, so filled with the Holy Spirit, and so responsible for people's needs that they are irreversibly drawn into the fast-moving currents of the congregational life.

We Must Write the New Chapter

Acts ends abruptly, like an unfinished symphony. I think that's exactly what Luke intended. He did not want to give the impression of the closing of an age but the beginning of the era of the Holy Spirit. His purpose for dramatizing the acts of the Holy Spirit, the birth of the Church, and strategy for changing the world is complete. More "chapters" have been written by other generations who dared to follow the Master. The newest chapter is being written by you and me.

The same power available to Paul and the early Church is available for us today through the Holy Spirit. The same miraculous life can become part of our everyday lives. The same kind of church can be born in your town. I pray that you will be gripped by the story of Acts and will never be the same. I hope that a bland, religious life will no longer be tolerable to you, and that you will be disturbed and alarmed by seeing the difference between the way things are and the way life and the Church are meant to be. As you continue the story and write new chapters, may you never be easily satisfied again. I believe that's exactly what Luke—and the Holy Spirit—want to accomplish.

Printed in the United States
by Baker & Taylor Publisher Services